Gousha

TEXAS

ROAD ATLAS
AND VISITOR'S GUIDE

TEXT: MARY T. MULKERIN / DESIGN: EDWARD P. O'DELL

Table of Contents

Information Sources	Inside Front Cover
Almanac of Facts	2
Natural Color Relief Map	2–3
Key Locator Map	3
State Maps	4–19
Index	20–21
City Maps	22–29

Austin, Amarillo, Beaumont, Corpus Christi, El Paso, Fort Worth, Dallas, Houston, Galveston, Lubbock, Midland, Odessa, Wichita Falls, San Antonio

Visitor's Guide	30–56
Discovering Texas	30
Texas Time–Line	31
Going to Town in Texas	34
Major League Sports	40
Half–Pint Texas: Childrens' Favorites	41
The Great Outdoors	42
Scenic Drives	44
Surprise: Texas Wineries	46
Crossing the Border	47
Food: Hot! Hot! Hot!	48
Fairs and Festivals	50

Spotlight: Live Music Roundup 54
by Casey Monahan, Director of the Texas Music Office, Texas Department of Commerce

Mileage Map .... **Inside Back Cover**

H.M. Gousha
Simon & Schuster Inc.
A Paramount Communications Company

© 1991 H.M. Gousha, a division of Simon & Schuster Inc., 15 Columbus Circle, New York, NY 10023. All rights reserved. This atlas, or any parts thereof, may not be reproduced in any manner without written permission from the publisher. The publisher and author assume no legal responsibility for the appreciation or depreciation in the value of any premises, commercial or otherwise, by reason of their inclusion or exclusion from this book. The information contained in this atlas is subject to change but was correct to the best knowledge of the publisher at the time of publication.

Texas
LONE STAR STATE

Capital	Austin
Nickname	Lone Star State
Motto	Friendship
Bird	Mockingbird
Tree	Pecan
Flower	Bluebonnet
Gemstone	Topaz
Dish	Chili
Song	"Texas, Our Texas"

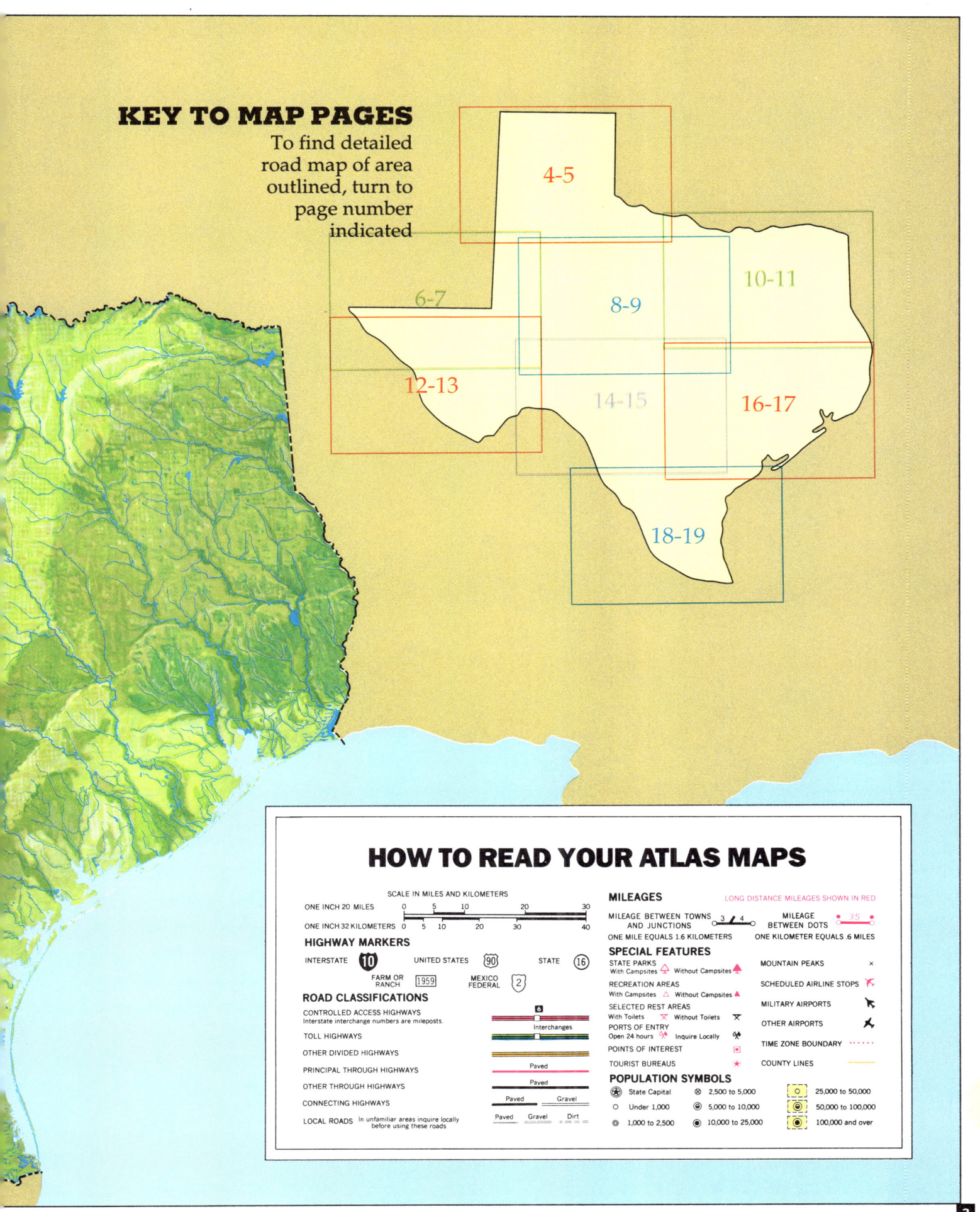

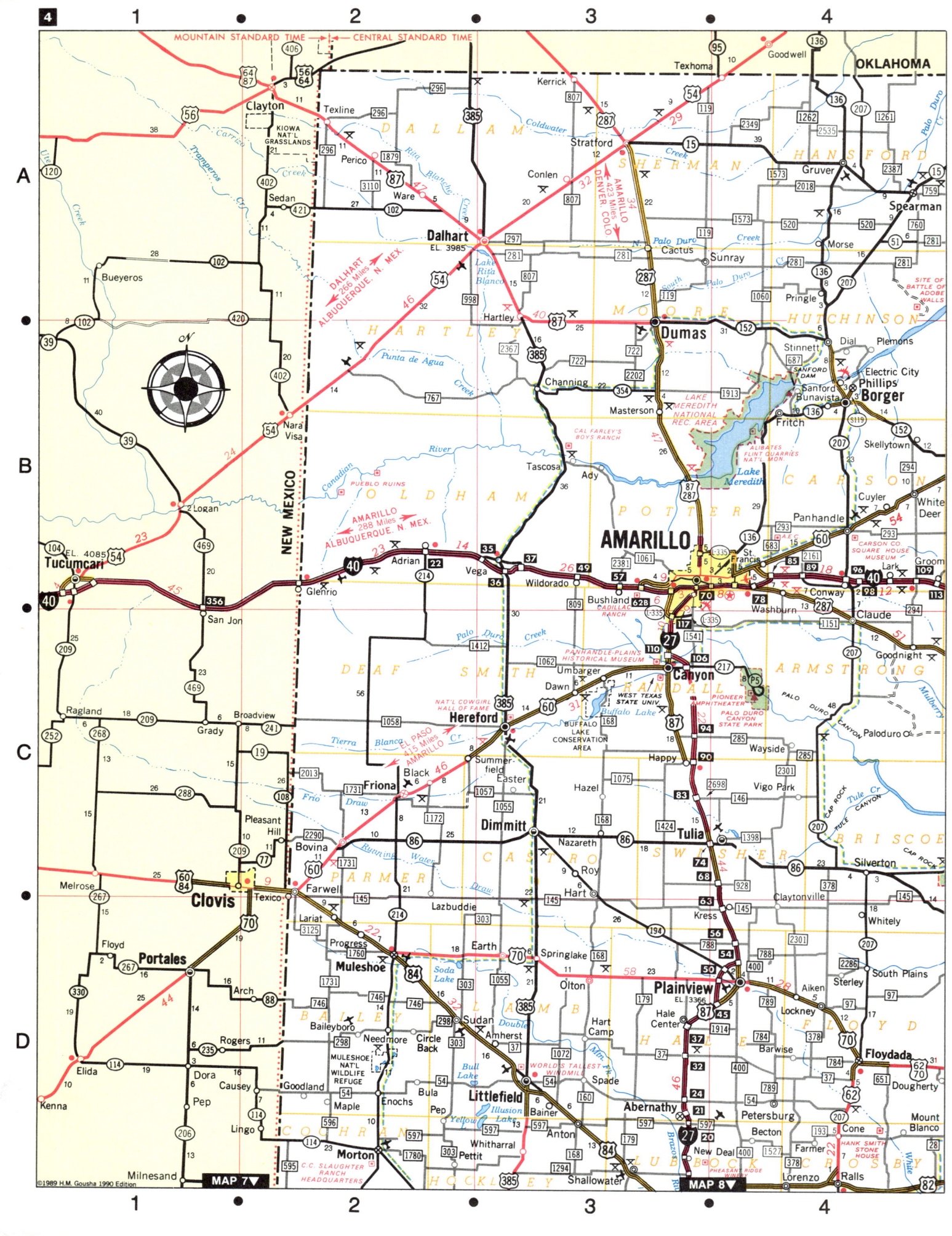

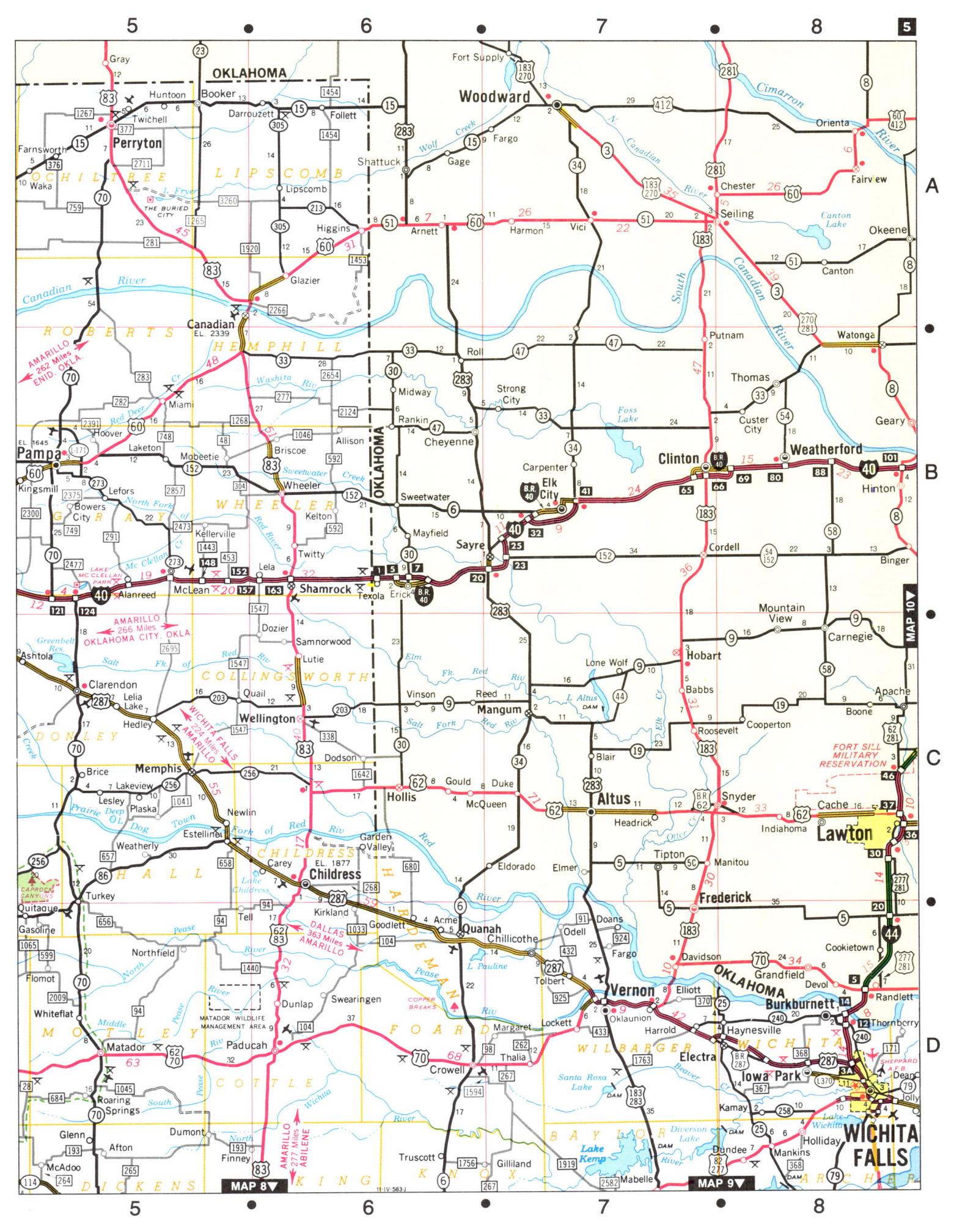

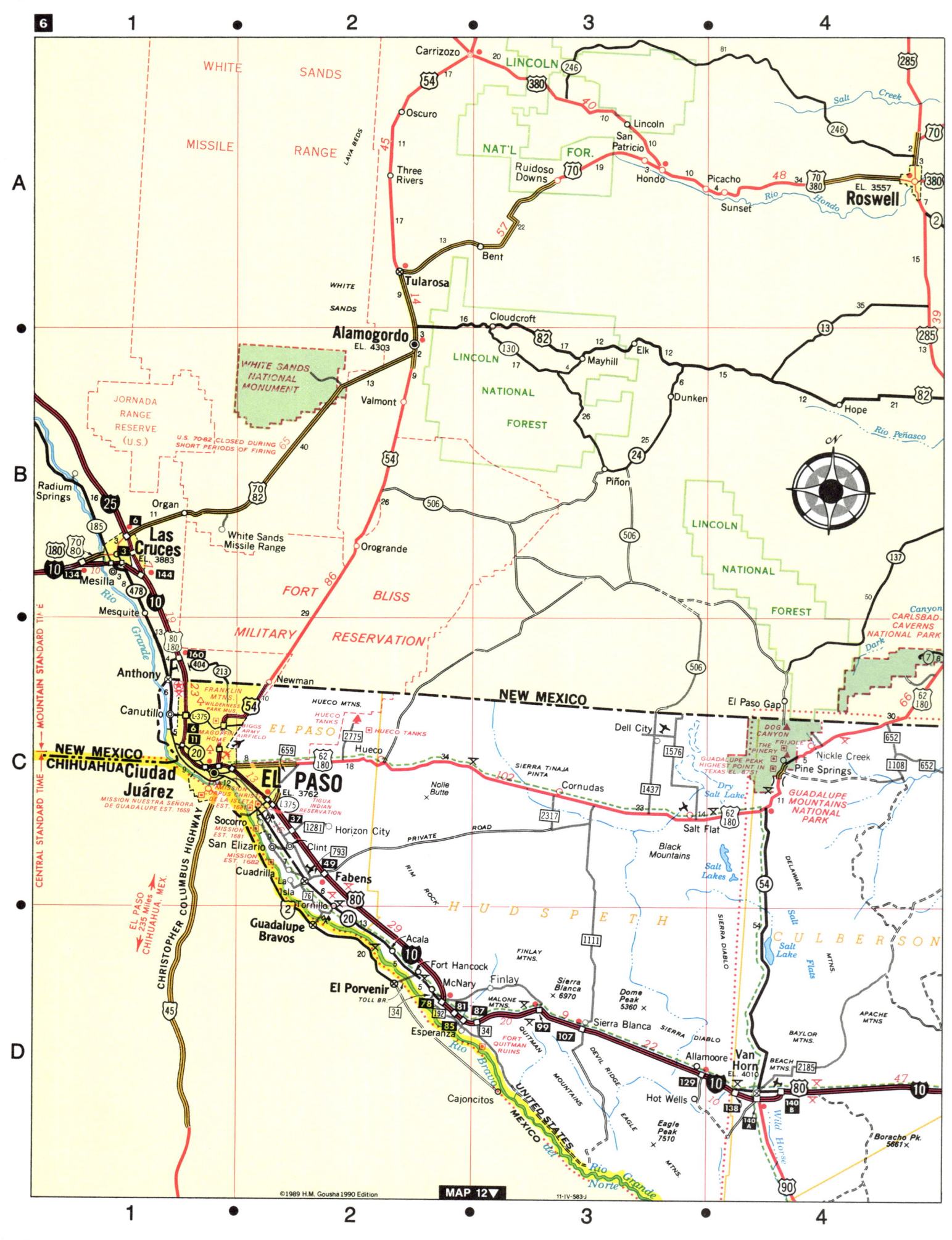

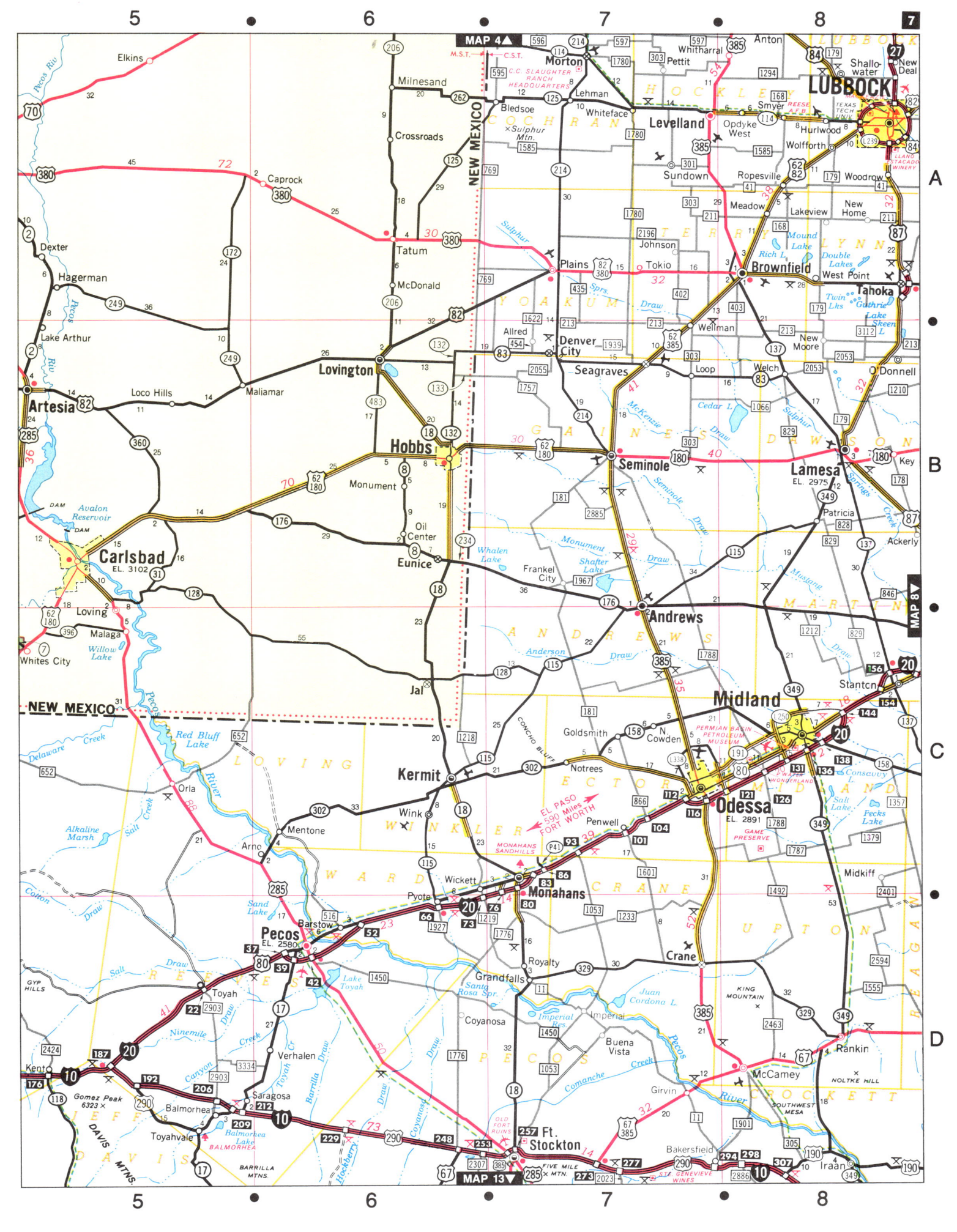

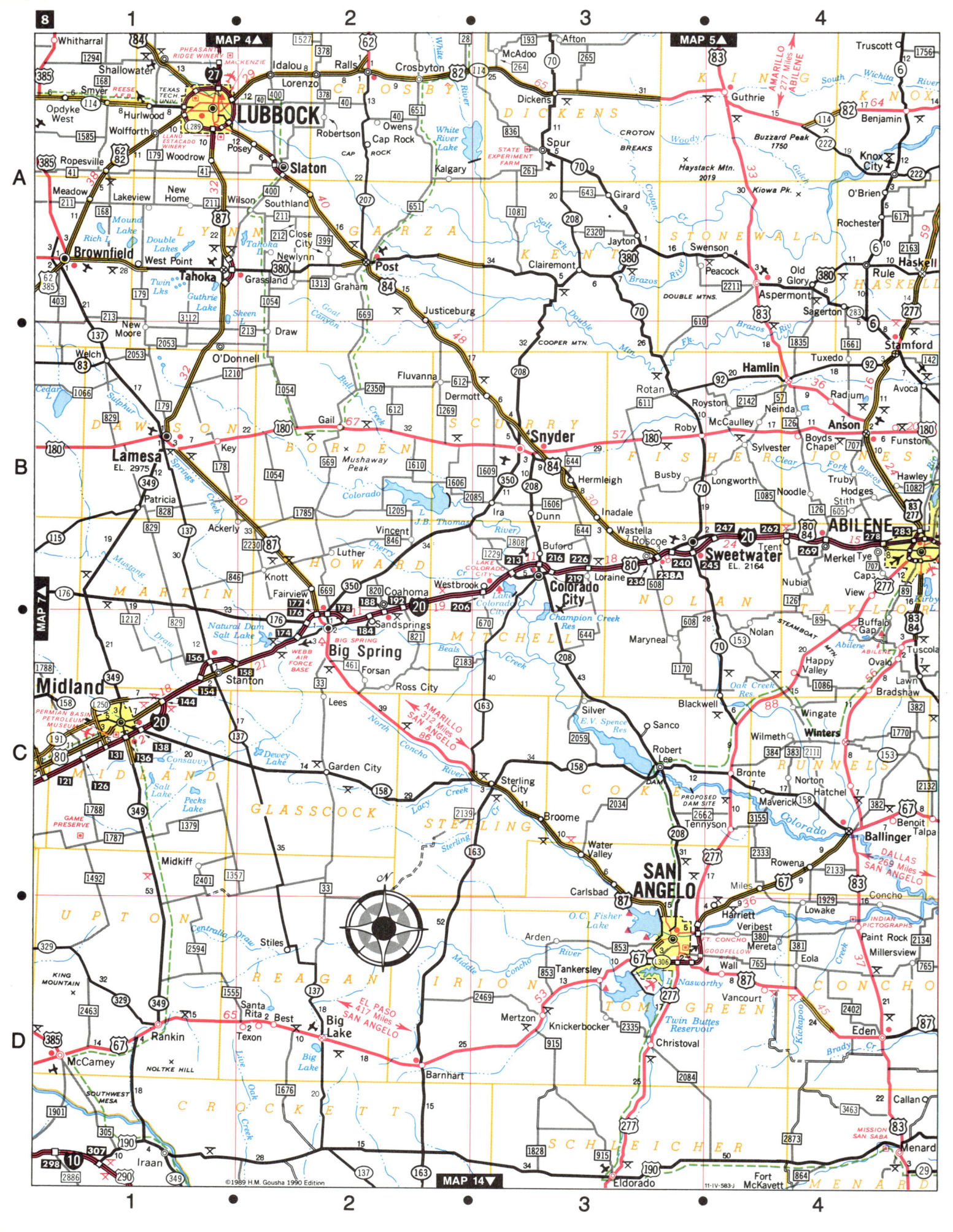

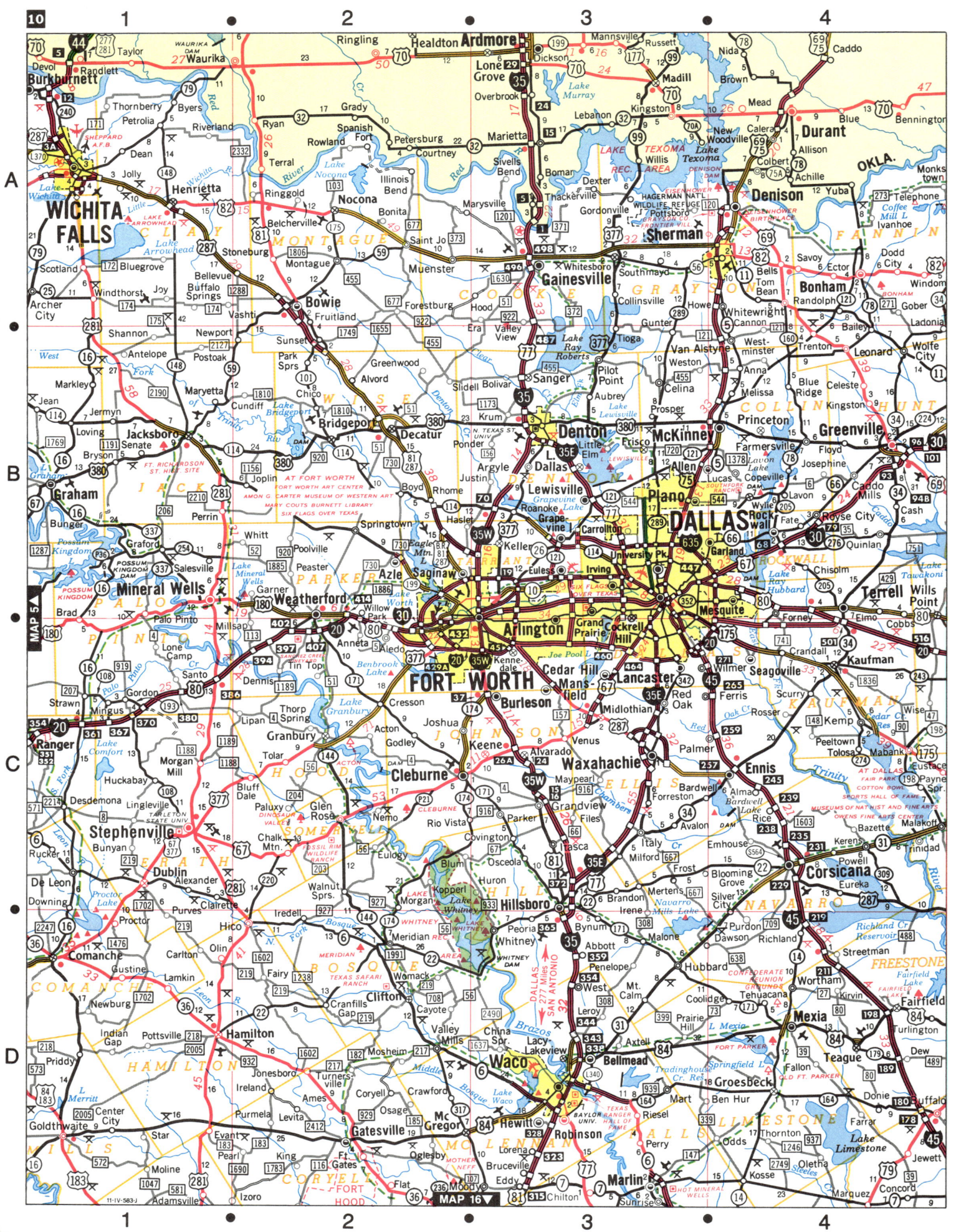

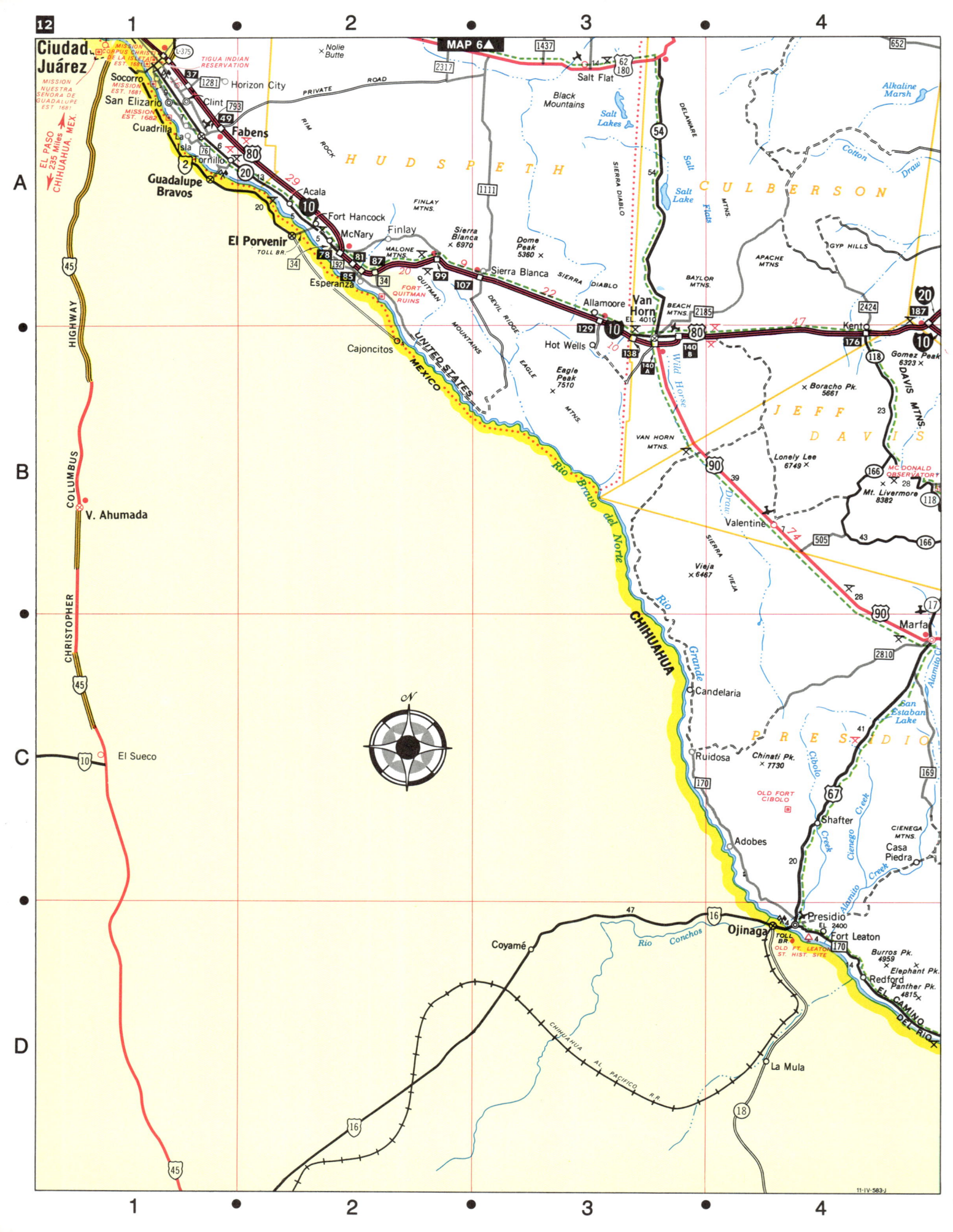

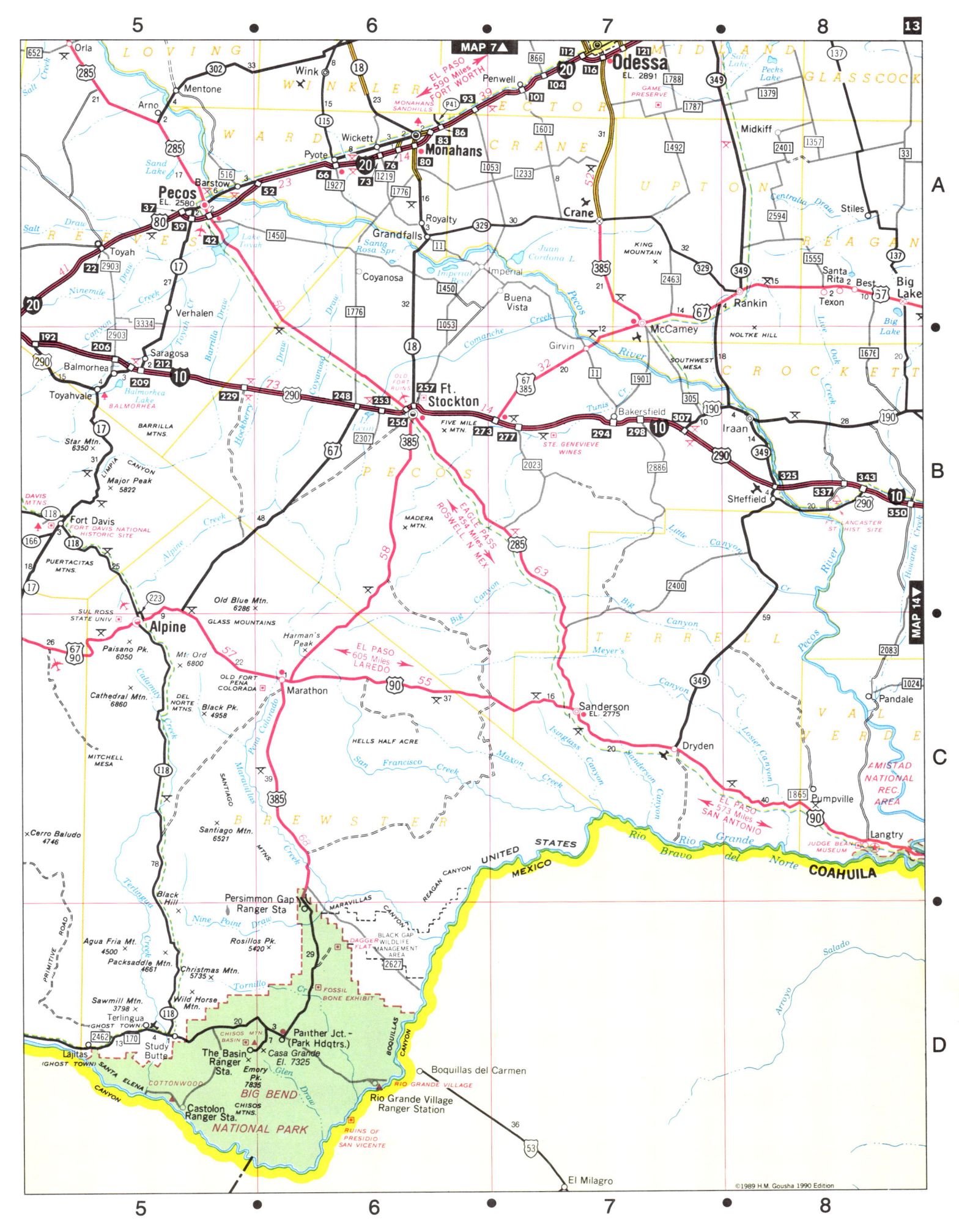

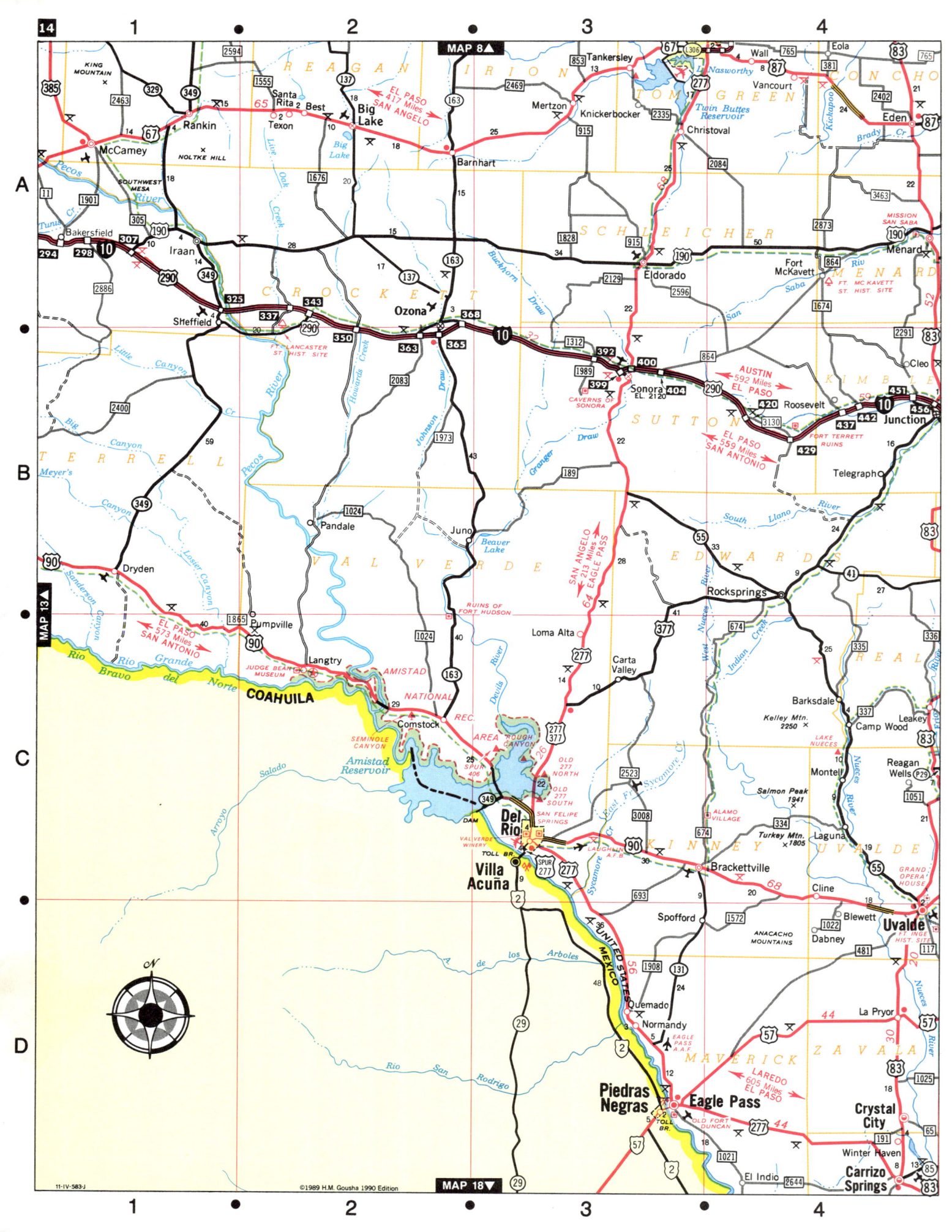

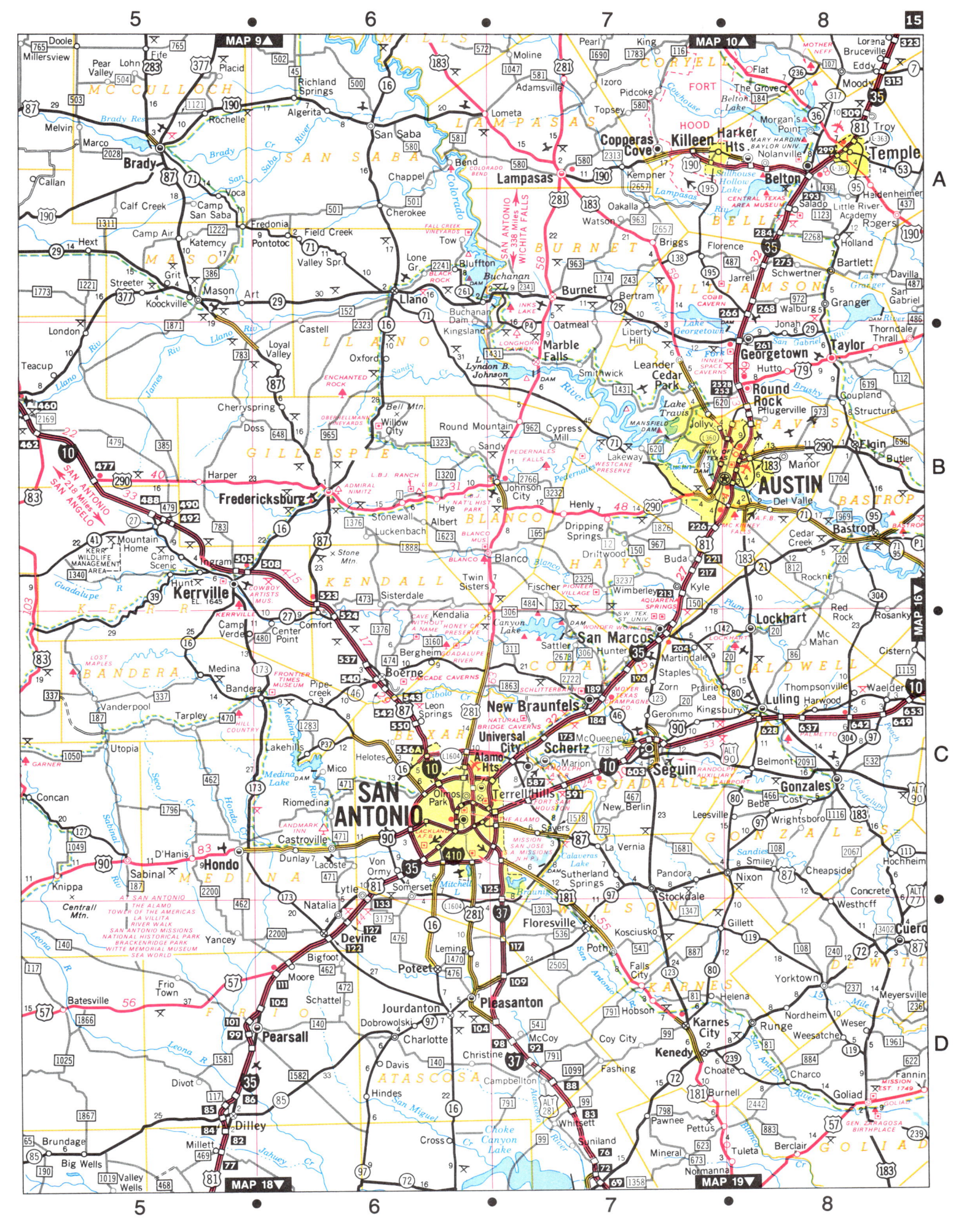

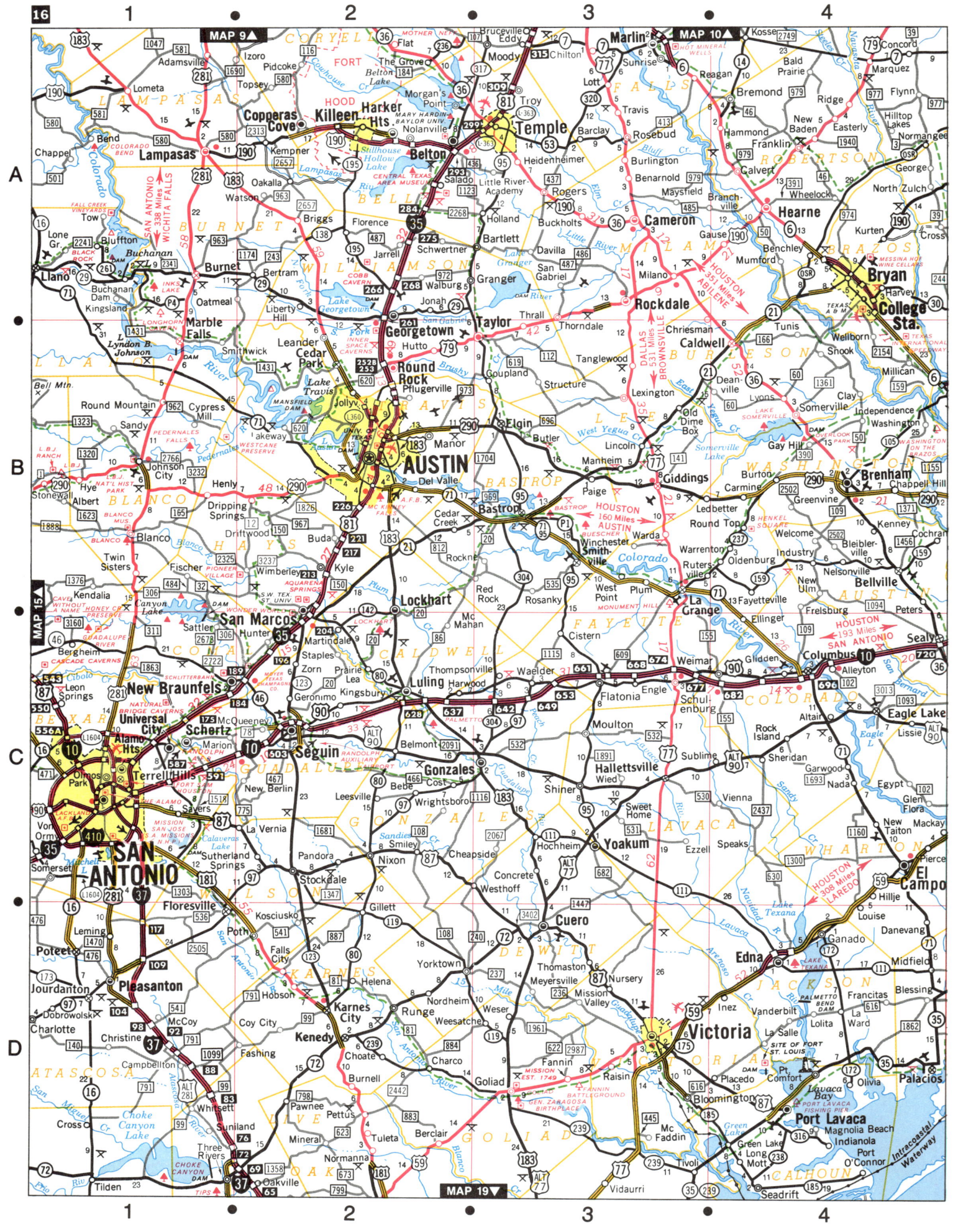

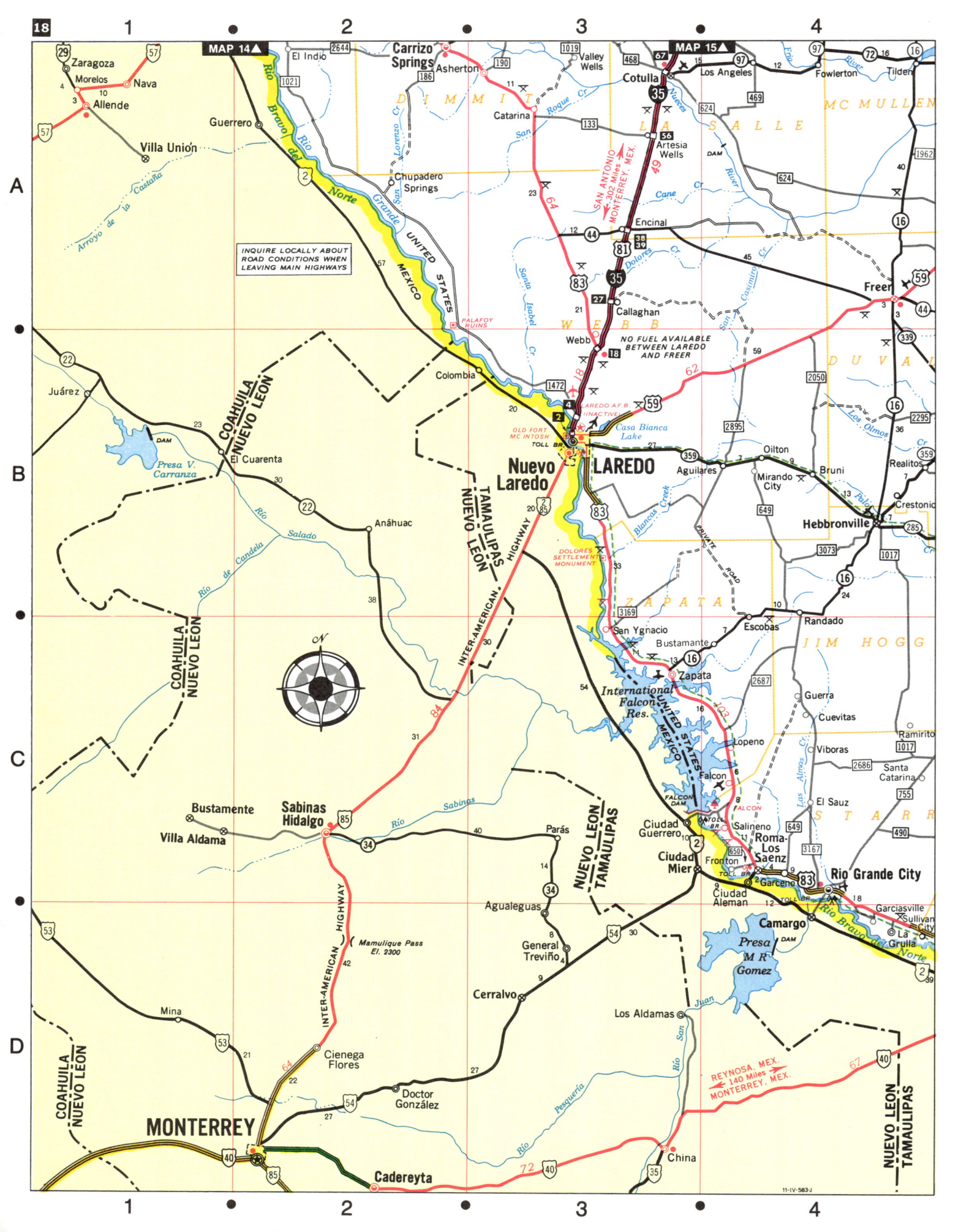

Place / Population / Page Grid
Alvin . . . . . 16,515 . . . . . 17-C6

TEXAS

Pop (1980) 14,228,283

Area 267,339 Sq. Mi.

COUNTIES

County	Co. Seat
Anderson	Palestine
Andrews	Andrews
Angelina	Lufkin
Aransas	Rockport
Archer	Archer City
Armstrong	Claude
Atascosa	Jourdanton
Austin	Bellville
Bailey	Muleshoe
Bandera	Bandera
Bastrop	Bastrop
Baylor	Seymour
Bee	Beeville
Bell	Belton
Bexar	San Antonio
Blanco	Johnson City
Borden	Gail
Bosque	Meridian
Bowie	Boston
Brazoria	Angleton
Brazos	Bryan
Brewster	Alpine
Briscoe	Silverton
Brooks	Falfurrias
Brown	Brownwood
Burleson	Caldwell
Burnet	Burnet
Caldwell	Lockhart
Calhoun	Port Lavaca
Callahan	Baird
Cameron	Brownsville
Camp	Pittsburg
Carson	Panhandle
Cass	Linden
Castro	Dimmitt
Chambers	Anahuac
Cherokee	Rusk
Childress	Childress
Clay	Henrietta
Cochran	Morton
Coke	Robert Lee
Coleman	Coleman
Collin	McKinney
Collingsworth	Wellington
Colorado	Columbus
Comal	New Braunfels
Comanche	Comanche
Concho	Paint Rock
Cooke	Gainsville
Coryell	Gatesville
Cottle	Paducah
Crane	Crane
Crockett	Ozona
Crosby	Crosbyton
Culberson	Van Horn
Dallam	Dalhart
Dallas	Dallas
Dawson	Lamesa
Deaf Smith	Hereford
Delta	Cooper
Denton	Denton
De Witt	Cuero
Dickens	Dickens
Dimmitt	Carrizo Springs
Donley	Claredon
Duval	San Diego
Eastland	Eastland
Ector	Odessa
Edwards	Rocksprings
Ellis	Waxahachie
El Paso	El Paso
Erath	Stephenville
Falls	Marlin
Fannin	Bonham
Fayette	La Grange
Fisher	Roby
Floyd	Folydada
Foard	Crowell
Fort Bend	Richmond
Franklin	Mount Vernon
Freestone	Fairfield
Frio	Pearsall
Gaines	Seminole
Galveston	Galveston
Garza	Post
Gillespie	Fredericksburg
Glasscock	Garden City
Goliad	Goliad
Gonzales	Gonzales
Gray	Pampa
Grayson	Sherman
Gregg	Longview
Grimes	Anderson
Guadalupe	Seguin
Hale	Plainview
Hall	Memphis
Hamilton	Hamilton
Hansford	Spearman
Hardeman	Quanah
Hardin	Kountze
Harris	Houston
Harrison	Marshall
Hartley	Channing
Haskell	Haskell
Hays	San Marcos
Hemphill	Canadian
Henderson	Athens
Hidalgo	Edinburg
Hill	Hillsboro
Hockley	Levelland
Hood	Granbury
Hopkins	Sulphur Springs
Houston	Crockett
Howard	Big Spring
Hudspeth	Sierra Blanca
Hunt	Greenville
Hutchinson	Stinnett
Irion	Mertzon
Jack	Jacksboro
Jackson	Edna
Jasper	Jasper
Jeff Davis	Fort Davis
Jefferson	Beaumont
Jim Hogg	Hebbronville
Jim Wells	Alice
Johnson	Cleburne
Jones	Anson
Karnes	Karnes City
Kaufman	Kaufman
Kendall	Boerne
Kenedy	Sarita
Kent	Jayton
Kerr	Kerrville
Kimble	Junction
King	Guthrie
Kinney	Brackettville
Kleberg	Kingsville
Knox	Benjamin
Lamar	Paris
Lamb	Littlefield
Lampasas	Lampasas
La Salle	Cotulla
Lavaca	Hallettsville
Lee	Giddings
Leon	Centerville
Liberty	Liberty
Limestone	Groesbeck
Lipscomb	Lipscomb
Live Oak	George West
Llano	Llano
Loving	Mentone
Lubbock	Lubbock
Lynn	Tahoka
Madison	Madisonville
Marion	Jefferson
Martin	Stanton
Mason	Mason
Matagorda	Bay City
Maverick	Eagle Pass
McCulloch	Brady
McLennan	Waco
McMullen	Tilden
Medina	Hondo
Menard	Menard
Midland	Midland
Milam	Cameron
Mills	Goldthwaite
Mitchell	Colorado City
Montague	Montague
Montgomery	Conroe
Moore	Dumas
Morris	Daingerfield
Motley	Matador
Nacogdoches	Nacogdoches
Navarro	Corsicana
Newton	Newton
Nolan	Sweetwater
Nueces	Corpus Christi
Ochiltree	Perryton
Oldham	Vega
Orange	Orange
Palo Pinto	Palo Pinto
Panola	Carthage
Parker	Weatherford
Parmer	Farwell
Pecos	Fort Stockton
Polk	Livingston
Potter	Amarillo
Presidio	Marfa
Rains	Emory
Randall	Canyon
Reagan	Big Lake
Real	Leakey
Red River	Clarksville
Reeves	Pecos
Refugio	Refugio
Roberts	Miami
Robertson	Franklin
Rockwall	Rockwall
Runnels	Ballinger
Rusk	Henderson
Sabine	Hemphill
San Augustine	San Augustine
San Jacinto	Coldspring
San Patricio	Sinton
San Saba	San Saba
Schleicher	Eldorado
Scurry	Snyder
Shackelford	Albany
Shelby	Center
Sherman	Stratford
Smith	Tyler
Somervell	Glen Rose
Starr	Rio Grande City
Stephens	Breckenridge
Sterling	Sterling City
Stonewall	Aspermont
Sutton	Sonora
Swisher	Tulia
Tarrant	Fort Worth
Taylor	Abilene
Terrell	Sanderson
Terry	Brownfield
Throckmorton	Throckmorton
Titus	Mount Pleasant
Tom Green	San Angelo
Travis	Austin
Trinity	Groveton
Tyler	Woodville
Upshur	Gilmer
Upton	Rankin
Uvalde	Uvalde
Val Verde	Del Rio
Van Zandt	Canton
Victoria	Victoria
Walker	Huntsville
Waller	Hempstead
Ward	Monahans
Washington	Brenham
Webb	Laredo
Wharton	Wharton
Wheeler	Wheeler
Wichita	Wichita Falls
Wilbarger	Vernon
Willacy	Raymondville
Williamson	Georgetown
Wilson	Floresville
Winkler	Kermit
Wise	Decatur
Wood	Quitman
Yoakum	Plains
Young	Graham
Zapata	Zapata
Zavala	Crystal City

COMPLETE LIST OF CITIES AND TOWNS

1980 Census
• County Seats

Abbott 359 . . . 9-C8
Abernathy 2,904 . . . 4-D3
Abilene • 98,315 . . . 8-B4
Acala . . . 6-D2
Ackerly 317 . . . 7-B8
Acme . . . 5-D6
Acton . . . 9-B7
Adamsville . . . 9-D7
Addison . . . 25-B6
Adkins . . . 29-D8
Admiral . . . 9-C5
Adobes . . . 12-C4
Adrian 222 . . . 4-B2
Ady . . . 4-B3
Afton . . . 5-D5
Agua Dulce 934 . . . 19-B5
Aguilares . . . 18-B3
Aiken . . . 11-D7
Aiken . . . 4-D4
Alamo 5,831 . . . 19-D5
Alamo Heights 6,252 . . . 15-C6,29-C6
Alanreed . . . 5-B5
Alba 568 . . . 11-B5
Albany • 2,450 . . . 9-B5
Albert . . . 15-B6
Aldine . . . 26-A2
Aledo 1,027 . . . 9-B7
Alexander . . . 9-C7
Alfred . . . 19-A5
Algerita . . . 9-D6
Alice • 20,961 . . . 19-B5
Allamoore . . . 6-D3
Allen 8,314 . . . 10-B3
Alleyton . . . 16-C4
Allison . . . 5-B6
Allred . . . 7-B7
Alma 171 . . . 10-C4
Almeda . . . 26-E2
Alpine . . . 13-C5
Altair . . . 16-C4
Alto . . . 11-D6
Alvarado 2,701 . . . 9-B8
Alvin 16,515 . . . 17-C6
Alvord 874 . . . 9-A7
Amarillo • 149,230 . . . 4-B3,23-B5
Ames . . . 17-B7
Ames . . . 9-D7
Amherst 971 . . . 4-D3
Anahauc • 1,840 . . . 17-B7
Anderson • . . . 17-B5
Andrews • 11,061 . . . 7-C7
Angleton • 13,929 . . . 17-C6
Anna 855 . . . 10-B4
Annarose . . . 19-A5
Anneta . . . 9-B7
Annona 471 . . . 11-A6
Anson • 2,831 . . . 8-B4
Antelope . . . 9-A6
Anton 1,181 . . . 4-D3
Appleby . . . 11-D7
Apple Springs . . . 11-D6
Aransas Pass 7,173 . . . 19-A7
Archer City • 1,862 . . . 9-A6
Arcola . . . 17-C5,26-F2
Arden . . . 8-D3
Argyle . . . 9-A8
Arlington 160,123 . . . 9-B8,24-D4
Arno . . . 7-C5
Arp 939 . . . 11-C6
Art . . . 15-A5
Artesia Wells . . . 18-A3
Arthur City . . . 11-A5
Asherton 1,574 . . . 18-A2
Ashtola . . . 5-C5
Ashwood . . . 17-C5
Aspermont • 1,357 . . . 8-A4
Atascosa . . . 29-E5
Athens • 10,197 . . . 11-C5
Atlanta 6,272 . . . 11-B7
Aubrey 948 . . . 10-B3
Austin • 345,496 . . . 15-B8,22-D3
Austonio . . . 17-A5
Austwell 280 . . . 19-A7
Avalon . . . 10-C3
Avery 520 . . . 11-A6
Avinger 671 . . . 11-B7
Avondale . . . 24-B1
Avoca . . . 8-B4
Axtell . . . 10-B3
Azle 5,822 . . . 9-B7
Bacliff . . . 17-C6,27-C6
Bagwell . . . 11-A6
Bailey . . . 10-B4
Baileyboro . . . 4-D2
Bainer . . . 4-D3
Baird • 1,696 . . . 9-B5
Bakersfield . . . 7-D8
Balch Springs 13,746 . . . 25-D8
Balcones Heights . . . 29-C6
Bald Prairie . . . 16-A4
Ballinger • 4,207 . . . 8-C4
Balmorhea 568 . . . 7-D5
Bandera • 947 . . . 15-C5
Bangs 1,716 . . . 9-C5
Banquete . . . 19-A5
Barclay . . . 16-A3
Bardwell . . . 10-C3
Barksdale . . . 14-C4
Barnhart . . . 8-D2
Barrett . . . 17-B6
Barstow 637 . . . 7-D6
Bartlett 1,567 . . . 9-D8
Barwise . . . 4-D4
Basin Ranger Station, The . . . 13-D5
Bassett . . . 11-B7
Bastrop • 3,789 . . . 15-B8
Batesville . . . 15-D5
Batson . . . 17-B7
Baxter . . . 11-C5
Bay City • 17,837 . . . 17-D5
Bayside . . . 19-A6
Baytown 56,923 . . . 17-C6,27-A6
Bazette . . . 10-C4
Beach City . . . 27-A7
Beasley 410 . . . 17-C5
Beaumont • 118,102 . . . 17-B7,23-B7
Beaumont Place . . . 26-C4
Bebe . . . 15-C8
Beckville 945 . . . 11-C7
Becton . . . 4-D4
Bedford 20,821 . . . 24-C4
Bedias . . . 17-A5
Bee Cave . . . 22-D1
Beech Grove . . . 17-A7
Beeville • 14,574 . . . 19-A6
Belk . . . 11-A5
Bellaire 14,950 . . . 26-D1
Bellevue 352 . . . 9-A7
Bellmead 7,569 . . . 10-D3
Bells 846 . . . 10-A4
Bellville • 2,860 . . . 16-B4
Belmont . . . 15-C8
Belton • 10,660 . . . 9-D8
Benarnold . . . 16-A3
Benavides 1,978 . . . 19-B5
Ben Bolt . . . 19-B5
Benbrook . . . 24-E1
Benchley . . . 16-A4
Bend . . . 9-D6
Ben Franklin • 257 . . . 11-A5
Ben Hur . . . 10-D4
Benjamin • 257 . . . 8-A4
Benoit . . . 8-C4
Ben Wheeler . . . 11-C5
Berclair . . . 15-D8
Bergheim . . . 15-C6
Bertram 824 . . . 15-A7
Bessmay . . . 17-B7
Best . . . 8-D2
Bettie . . . 11-B6
Bevil Oaks . . . 17-B7
Biardstown . . . 11-A5
Bigfoot . . . 15-D6
Big Lake • 3,404 . . . 8-D2
Big Sandy 1,258 . . . 11-C6
Big Spring • 24,804 . . . 8-C2
Big Wells 939 . . . 15-D5
Birthright . . . 11-B5
Bishop 3,706 . . . 19-B5
Bivins . . . 11-B7
Black . . . 4-C2
Blackwell 286 . . . 8-C3
Blanco 1,179 . . . 15-B7
Blanket 388 . . . 9-C6
Bledsoe . . . 7-A7
Bleiberville . . . 16-B4
Blessing . . . 16-D4
Blewett . . . 14-D4
Bloomburg 419 . . . 11-B7
Blooming Grove 823 . . . 10-C4
Bloomington . . . 16-D3
Blossom 1,487 . . . 11-A5
Bluegrove . . . 9-A6
Blue Mound 2,169 . . . 24-C2
Blue Ridge 442 . . . 10-B4
Bluff Dale . . . 9-B7
Bluff Springs . . . 22-F3
Bluffton . . . 9-D6
Blum 357 . . . 9-C8
Boerne • 3,229 . . . 15-C6
Boerne • 3,229 . . . 29-A5
Bogata 1,508 . . . 11-A6
Boling . . . 17-C5
Bolivar . . . 9-A8
Bomarten . . . 9-A5
Bonham • 7,338 . . . 10-A4
Bonita . . . 10-A2
Bon Weir . . . 17-A7
Booker 1,219 . . . 5-A6
Borger 15,837 . . . 4-B4
Boston • . . . 11-A7
Bovina 1,499 . . . 4-C2
Bowers . . . 5-B5
Bowie 5,610 . . . 9-A7
Boxelder . . . 11-A6
Boyd 889 . . . 9-A8
Boyds Chapel . . . 8-B4
Brackettville • 1,676 . . . 14-C4
Brad . . . 9-B6
Bradshaw . . . 8-C4
Brady • 5,969 . . . 9-D5
Branchville . . . 16-A4
Brandon . . . 10-C3
Brashear . . . 11-B5
Brazoria 3,025 . . . 17-D5
Breckenridge • 6,921 . . . 9-B5
Bremond 1,025 . . . 16-A4
Brenham • 10,966 . . . 16-B4
Brice . . . 5-C5
Bridge City 7,667 . . . 17-B8
Bridgeport 3,737 . . . 9-A7
Briggs . . . 9-D7
Briscoe . . . 5-B6
Broaddus 225 . . . 11-D7
Bronson 254 . . . 11-D8
Bronte 983 . . . 8-C4
Brookeland . . . 11-D8
Brookesmith . . . 9-D5
Brookshire 2,175 . . . 17-C5
Brookside Village 1,453 . . . 26-E3
Brookston . . . 11-A5
Broome . . . 8-C3
Brownfield • 10,387 . . . 7-A8
Brownsboro 582 . . . 11-C5
Brownsville • 84,997 . . . 19-D6
Brownwood • 19,203 . . . 9-C5
Bruceville . . . 9-D8
Brundage . . . 15-D5
Bruni . . . 18-B4
Bryan • 44,337 . . . 16-A4
Bryson 579 . . . 9-A6
Buchanan Dam . . . 15-A6
Buckholts 388 . . . 16-A3
Buckingham . . . 25-B7
Buda 597 . . . 15-B7
Buena Vista . . . 7-D7
Buffalo 1,507 . . . 10-D4
Buffalo Gap 387 . . . 8-C4
Buffalo Springs . . . 9-A7
Buford . . . 8-B3
Bula . . . 4-D2
Bullard 681 . . . 11-C5
Bulverde . . . 29-A6
Buna . . . 17-B8
Bunavista . . . 4-B4
Bunger . . . 9-B6
Bunker Hill 3,750 . . . 26-C1
Bunyan . . . 9-C6
Burkburnett 10,668 . . . 5-D8
Burke 322 . . . 11-D6
Burkett . . . 9-C5
Burkeville . . . 17-A7
Burleson 11,734 . . . 9-B8,24-F2
Burlington . . . 16-A3
Burnell . . . 15-D7
Burnet • 3,410 . . . 15-A7
Burton 325 . . . 16-B4
Busby . . . 8-B3
Bushland . . . 4-B3
Bustamante . . . 18-C3
Butler . . . 15-B8
Byers 556 . . . 10-A1
Bynum 232 . . . 9-C8
Byrds . . . 9-C5
Cactus . . . 4-A3
Caddo . . . 9-B6
Caddo Mills 1,060 . . . 10-B4
Caldwell • 2,953 . . . 16-B3
Calf Creek . . . 9-D5
Callaghan . . . 18-A3
Callan . . . 8-D4
Call Junction . . . 17-A8
Calvert 1,732 . . . 16-A4
Camden . . . 17-A6
Cameron • 5,721 . . . 16-A3
Camp Air . . . 9-D5
Campbell 549 . . . 10-B4
Campbellton . . . 15-D6
Camp Ruby . . . 17-A6
Camp San Saba . . . 9-D5
Camp Scenic . . . 15-B5
Camp Seale . . . 17-A7
Camp Verde . . . 15-C5
Camp Wood 728 . . . 14-C4
Canada Verde . . . 29-E7
Canadian • 3,491 . . . 5-A5
Candelaria . . . 12-C3
Cannon . . . 10-A4
Canton • 2,845 . . . 11-C5
Canutillo . . . 6-C1
Canyon • 10,724 . . . 4-C3
Cap Rock . . . 8-A2
Caps . . . 8-B4
Carbon 281 . . . 9-C6
Carey . . . 5-C6
Carlisle . . . 17-A6
Carlos . . . 17-B5
Carlsbad . . . 8-C3
Carlton . . . 9-C7
Carmine 239 . . . 16-B4
Carrizo Springs • 6,886 . . . 14-D4
Carrollton 40,591 . . . 10-B3,25-B6
Carta Valley . . . 14-C3
Carthage • 6,447 . . . 11-C7
Casa Piedra . . . 12-C4
Cash . . . 10-B4
Cason . . . 11-B6
Castalon Ranger Station . . . 13-D5
Castell . . . 15-B6
Castle Hills . . . 29-C6
Castroville 1,821 . . . 15-C6
Catarina . . . 18-A3
Cayote . . . 9-C8
Cayuga . . . 11-C5
Cedar Creek . . . 15-B8
Cedar Hill 6,849 . . . 9-B8,25-F5
Cedar Lane . . . 17-D5
Cedar Park . . . 15-B7,22-B2
Celeste 716 . . . 10-B4
Celina 1,520 . . . 10-B3
Center • 5,827 . . . 11-D7
Center City . . . 9-D6
Center Point . . . 15-C6
Centerville . . . 11-D6
Centerville • 799 . . . 11-D5
Central . . . 11-D6
Centralia . . . 11-D6
Chalk Hill . . . 11-C6
Chalk Mountain . . . 9-C7
Chandler 1,308 . . . 11-C5
Channing • 304 . . . 4-B3
Chapman . . . 11-C6
Chapman Ranch . . . 19-B6
Chappel . . . 9-D6
Chappell Hill . . . 16-B4
Charco . . . 15-D8
Charleston . . . 11-B5
Charlotte 1,443 . . . 15-D6
Cheapside . . . 15-C8
Cheek . . . 17-B7
Cherokee . . . 9-D6
Cherryspring . . . 15-B5
Chester . . . 17-A7
Chico 890 . . . 9-A7
Chicota . . . 11-A5
Childress • 5,817 . . . 5-C6
Chillicothe 1,052 . . . 5-D7
Chilton . . . 9-D8
China 1,351 . . . 17-B7
China Grove . . . 29-D7
China Springs . . . 9-C8
Chireno 371 . . . 11-D7
Chisholm . . . 10-B4
Choate . . . 15-D7
Chriesman . . . 16-B3
Christine 392 . . . 15-D6
Christoval . . . 8-D3
Chupadero Springs . . . 18-A2
Cibolo . . . 29-B8
Circle Back . . . 4-D2
Circleville . . . 22-E1
Cisco 4,517 . . . 9-B5
Cistern . . . 16-C3
Clairemont . . . 8-A3
Clairette . . . 9-C7
Clarendon • 2,220 . . . 5-C5
Clareville . . . 19-A5
Clarksville • 4,917 . . . 11-A5
Claude • 1,112 . . . 4-C4
Clawson . . . 11-D6
Clay . . . 16-B4
Clayton . . . 11-C7
Claytonville . . . 4-C4
Clear Lake Shores . . . 27-C6
Cleburne • 19,218 . . . 9-B8
Clegg . . . 19-A5
Cleo . . . 14-B4
Cleveland 5,977 . . . 17-B6
Clifton 3,063 . . . 9-C7
Cline . . . 14-C4
Clint 1,314 . . . 6-C2
Clodine . . . 17-C5
Close City . . . 8-A2
Cloverleaf . . . 26-C4
Clute 9,577 . . . 17-D6
Clyde 2,562 . . . 9-B5
Coahoma 1,069 . . . 8-B2
Cobbs . . . 10-C4
Cockrell Hill 3,262 . . . 10-C3,25-D6
Cochran . . . 16-B4
Coke . . . 11-B5
Coldspring • 569 . . . 17-A6
Coleman • 5,960 . . . 9-C5
Collegeport . . . 17-D5
College Station 37,272 . . . 16-A4
Colleyville 6,700 . . . 24-C4
Collinsville 860 . . . 10-A3
Colmesnell 553 . . . 17-A7
Colorado City • 5,405 . . . 8-B3
Colton . . . 22-F3
Columbus • 3,923 . . . 16-C4
Comanche • 4,075 . . . 9-C6
Combes 1,441 . . . 19-D6
Comfort . . . 15-C6
Commerce 8,136 . . . 10-B4
Como 554 . . . 11-B5
Comstock . . . 14-C2
Concan . . . 15-C5
Concepcion . . . 19-B5
Concho . . . 8-C4
Concord . . . 11-D7
Concord . . . 16-A4
Concrete . . . 15-C8
Cone . . . 4-D4
Conlen . . . 4-A3
Conroe • 18,034 . . . 17-B5
Converse . . . 29-C7
Conway . . . 4-B4
Cookville . . . 11-B6
Coolidge 810 . . . 10-D3
Cooper • 2,338 . . . 11-B5
Copeville . . . 10-B4
Coppell . . . 25-B5
Copperas Cove 19,469 . . . 9-D7
Corinth . . . 11-D5
Corley . . . 11-B7
Cornudas . . . 6-C3
Corpus Christi • 231,999 . . . 19-A6,23-E6
Corrigan 1,770 . . . 17-A6
Corsicana • 21,712 . . . 10-C4
Coryell . . . 9-C7
Cost . . . 15-C8
Cottonwood . . . 9-C5
Cotulla • 3,912 . . . 18-A3
Coupland . . . 15-B8
Courtney . . . 17-B5
Cove . . . 17-B6
Covington 259 . . . 9-C8
Coyanosa . . . 7-D6
Coy City . . . 15-D7
Crabbs Prairie . . . 17-A5
Craig . . . 11-C6
Crandell 831 . . . 10-C4
Crane • 3,622 . . . 7-D7
Cranfills Gap 341 . . . 9-C7
Crawford 610 . . . 9-C8
Cresson . . . 9-B8
Crestonio . . . 18-B4
Crockett • 7,405 . . . 11-D5
Crosby . . . 17-B6
Crosbytown • 2,289 . . . 4-D4
Cross . . . 15-D6
Cross Cut . . . 9-C5
Cross Plains 1,240 . . . 9-C5
Cross Roads . . . 11-C5
Cross Roads . . . 17-A5
Crow . . . 11-C5
Crowell • 1,509 . . . 5-D6
Crowley . . . 24-F2
Crystal City • 8,334 . . . 14-D4
Crystal Falls . . . 9-B5
Cuadrilla . . . 6-C2
Cuero • 7,124 . . . 15-D8
Cuevitas . . . 18-C4
Cumby 647 . . . 11-B5
Cundiff . . . 9-A7
Cuney . . . 11-C5
Cunningham . . . 11-B5
Cushing 518 . . . 11-D6
Cuyler . . . 4-B4
Cypress . . . 17-B5
Cypress Mill . . . 15-B7
Dabney . . . 14-D4
Daingerfield • 3,030 . . . 11-B6
Daisetta 1,177 . . . 17-B7
Dalby Springs . . . 11-A6
Dalhart • 6,854 . . . 4-A2
Dallas • 904,078 . . . 10-B3,25-D7
Dalworthington Gardens . . . 24-E3
Damon . . . 17-C5
Danevang . . . 16-D4
Darco . . . 11-C7
Darrouzett 444 . . . 5-A6
Davilla . . . 15-A8
Davis . . . 15-D6
Dawn . . . 4-C3
Dawson 747 . . . 10-D4
Dayton 4,908 . . . 17-B6
Deadwood . . . 11-C7
Dean . . . 10-A1
Deanville . . . 16-B4
De Berry . . . 11-C7
Decatur • 4,104 . . . 9-A8
Deer Park . . . 27-A5
De Kalb 2,217 . . . 11-A6
De Leon 2,478 . . . 9-C6
Dell City . . . 6-C3
Del Rio • 30,034 . . . 14-C3
Del Valle . . . 15-B8,22-E4
Denison 23,884 . . . 10-A4
Denning . . . 11-D7
Dennis . . . 9-B7
Denton • 48,063 . . . 9-A8
Denton Community . . . 9-C5
Denver City 4,704 . . . 7-B7
Deport 724 . . . 11-A5
Dermott . . . 8-B2
Desdemona . . . 9-C6
De Soto 15,538 . . . 25-F6
Dessau . . . 22-C4
Detroit 805 . . . 11-A5
Devers 507 . . . 17-B7
Devine 3,756 . . . 15-D6
Dew . . . 10-D4
Deweyville . . . 17-B8
Dexter . . . 10-A3
D'Hannis . . . 15-C5
Dial . . . 4-B4
Dialville . . . 11-D6
Diana . . . 11-B6
Diboll 5,227 . . . 17-A6
Dickens • 409 . . . 8-A3
Dickinson 7,505 . . . 17-C6,27-D6
Dido . . . 24-B1
Dilley 2,579 . . . 15-D5
Dimmitt • 5,019 . . . 4-C3
Dinero . . . 19-A5
Direct . . . 11-A5
Divot . . . 15-D5
Doans . . . 5-D7
Dobbin . . . 17-B5
Dobrowolski . . . 15-D6
Dodd City 286 . . . 10-A4
Dodson 185 . . . 5-C6
Donie . . . 10-D4
Donna 9,952 . . . 19-D5
Doole . . . 9-D5
Doss . . . 15-B5
Double Bayou . . . 17-C7
Doucette . . . 17-A7
Dougherty . . . 4-D4
Douglass . . . 11-D6
Douglassville . . . 11-B7
Downing . . . 9-C6
Dozier . . . 5-C6
Draw . . . 8-B2
Driftwood . . . 15-B7
Dripping Springs . . . 15-B7
Driscoll 648 . . . 19-B6
Dryden . . . 13-C7
Dublin 2,723 . . . 9-C7
Dumas • 12,194 . . . 4-B3
Dumont . . . 5-D5
Duncanville 27,781 . . . 25-E6
Dundee . . . 5-D7
Dunlap . . . 5-D6
Dunlay . . . 15-C6
Dunn . . . 8-B3
Dyersdale . . . 26-B3
Eagle Lake 3,921 . . . 16-C4
Eagle Pass • 21,407 . . . 14-D3
Early 2,313 . . . 9-C6
Earth 1,512 . . . 4-D3
East Bernard . . . 17-C5
East Columbia . . . 17-C5
Easter . . . 4-C3
Easterly . . . 16-A4
Eastland • 3,747 . . . 9-B6
Ector 573 . . . 10-A4
Edouch 3,092 . . . 19-D5
Eddy . . . 9-D8
Eden 1,294 . . . 8-D4
Edgecliff Village . . . 24-E2
Edgewood 1,413 . . . 11-C5
Edinburg • 24,075 . . . 19-C5
Edna • 5,650 . . . 16-D4
Edom 250 . . . 11-C5
Edroy . . . 19-A6
Egypt . . . 16-C4
Elbert . . . 9-A5
El Campo • 10,462 . . . 16-C4
Eldorado • 2,061 . . . 8-D3
Electra 3,755 . . . 5-D7
Electric City . . . 4-B4
Elgin 4,535 . . . 15-B8
Eliasville . . . 9-B6
El Indio . . . 14-D4
Elkhart 1,317 . . . 11-D5
El Lago . . . 27-C6
Ellinger . . . 16-C4
Elmaton . . . 17-D5
Elmendorf . . . 29-E7
Elmo . . . 10-B4
El Paso • 425,259 . . . 6-C2,23-E8
Elsa 5,061 . . . 19-D5
El Sauz . . . 18-C4
Elwood . . . 17-A5
Elysian Fields . . . 11-C7
Emhouse . . . 10-C4
Emory • 813 . . . 11-B5
Encinal 704 . . . 18-A3
Encino . . . 19-C5
Engle . . . 16-C3
English . . . 11-A6
Ennis 12,110 . . . 10-C4
Enochs . . . 4-D2
Eola . . . 8-D4
Eolian . . . 9-B5
Era . . . 9-A8
Escobas . . . 18-C4
Esperanza . . . 17-B5
Esperanza . . . 6-D2
Estelline 258 . . . 5-C5
Etoile . . . 11-D7
Euless 24,002 . . . 9-B8,24-C4
Eulogy . . . 9-C7
Eureka . . . 10-C4
Eustace 541 . . . 10-C4
Evadale . . . 17-B8
Evant 425 . . . 9-D7
Everman 5,387 . . . 24-E3
Ezzell . . . 16-C3
Fabens . . . 6-C2
Fainsworth . . . 5-A5
Fairfield • 3,505 . . . 10-D4
Fairview . . . 8-B2
Fairview . . . 29-F7
Fairy . . . 9-C7
Falcon . . . 18-C4
Falfurrias • 6,103 . . . 19-B5
Fallon . . . 10-D4
Falls City 580 . . . 15-D7
Fannett . . . 17-B7
Fannin . . . 15-D8
Fargo . . . 5-D7
Farmer . . . 4-D4
Farmers Branch 24,863 . . . 25-B6
Farmersville 2,360 . . . 10-B4
Farrar . . . 10-D4
Farrsville . . . 17-A7
Farwell • 1,354 . . . 4-C2
Fashing . . . 15-D7
Fate . . . 10-B4
Faught . . . 11-A5
Fauna . . . 26-B4
Faulkner . . . 11-A5
Fayatteville 356 . . . 16-B4
Faysville . . . 19-C5
Ferris 2,228 . . . 10-C4,25-F8
Field Creek . . . 9-D6
Fife . . . 9-D5
Files . . . 9-C8
Finlay . . . 6-D3
Finney . . . 5-D5
Fischer . . . 15-B7
Fisk . . . 9-C5
Flatonia 1,070 . . . 16-C3
Flomot . . . 5-D5
Florence 744 . . . 9-D7
Floresville • 4,381 . . . 15-D7,29-F7
Flower Mound . . . 24-A4
Floyd . . . 10-B4
Floydada • 4,193 . . . 4-D4
Fluvanna . . . 8-B2
Flynn . . . 16-A4
Follett 547 . . . 5-A6
Forestburg . . . 9-A8
Forest Hill . . . 24-E3
Forney 2,483 . . . 10-B4
Forreston . . . 10-C3
Forsan 239 . . . 8-C2
Fort Davis • . . . 13-B5
Fort Gates . . . 9-D7
Fort Hancock . . . 6-D2
Fort Leaton . . . 12-D4
Fort McKavett . . . 8-D4
Fort Stockton • 8,688 . . . 7-D7
Fort Worth • 385,141 . . . 9-B8,24-D3
Fostoria . . . 17-B6
Four Corners . . . 17-B6
Fowlerton . . . 18-A4
Francitas . . . 16-D4
Frankel City . . . 7-B7
Franklin • 1,349 . . . 16-A4
Frankston 1,255 . . . 11-C5
Fred . . . 17-A7
Fredericksburg • 6,412 . . . 15-B5
Fredonia . . . 9-D5
Freeport 13,444 . . . 17-D6
Freer 3,213 . . . 18-A4
Frelsburg . . . 16-B4
Fresno . . . 26-F2
Friday . . . 17-A6
Frio Town . . . 15-D5
Friona 3,809 . . . 4-C2
Frisco 3,420 . . . 10-B3
Fritch 2,299 . . . 4-B4
Frost 564 . . . 10-C3
Fruitland . . . 9-A7
Fruitvale . . . 11-B5
Frye . . . 9-C5
Fulbright . . . 11-A5
Fuller Springs . . . 11-D7
Fulshear 594 . . . 17-C5
Fulton 725 . . . 19-A7
Funston . . . 8-B4
Gail • . . . 8-B2
Gainesville • 14,081 . . . 9-A8
Galena Park . . . 26-C3
Gallatin . . . 11-D6
Galveston • 61,902 . . . 17-C7,27-F8
Ganado 1,770 . . . 16-D4
Garcerro . . . 18-C4
Garciasville . . . 18-D4
Garden City • . . . 8-C2
Garden Ridge . . . 29-B7
Garden Valley . . . 11-C5
Garden Valley . . . 5-C6
Garland 138,857 . . . 10-B4,25-B8
Garner . . . 9-B7
Garrison 1,059 . . . 11-D7
Garwood . . . 16-C4
Gasoline . . . 5-D5
Gatesville • 6,260 . . . 9-D7
Gause . . . 16-A3
Gay Hill . . . 16-B4
Geneva . . . 11-D8
George . . . 16-A4
Georgetown • 9,468 . . . 15-B8
George West • 2,627 . . . 19-A5
Geronimo . . . 15-C7
Giddings • 3,950 . . . 16-B3
Gilchrist . . . 17-C7
Gill . . . 11-C7
Gillett . . . 15-D8
Gilliland . . . 5-D7
Gilmer • 5,167 . . . 11-B6
Girard . . . 8-A3
Girvin . . . 7-D7
Gladewater 6,548 . . . 11-C6
Glazier . . . 5-A6
Glen Cove . . . 9-C5,27-C6
Glendale . . . 17-A6
Glen Flora . . . 16-C4
Glenn . . . 5-D5
Glenn Heights . . . 25-F6
Glen Rose • 2,075 . . . 9-C7
Glidden . . . 16-C4
Globe . . . 11-A5
Gober . . . 10-A4
Godley 614 . . . 9-B8
Goldboro . . . 9-C5
Goldsmith 409 . . . 7-C7
Goldthwaite • 1,783 . . . 9-D6
Goliad • 1,990 . . . 15-D8
Gonzales • 7,152 . . . 15-C8
Goodland . . . 4-D2
Goodlet . . . 5-D6
Goodnight . . . 4-C4
Goodrich 350 . . . 17-A6
Gordon 516 . . . 9-B6
Gordonville . . . 10-A3
Goree 524 . . . 9-A5
Gorman 1,258 . . . 9-C6
Graford 495 . . . 9-B6
Graham . . . 8-A2
Graham • 9,055 . . . 9-A6
Granbury • 3,332 . . . 9-B7
Grandfalls 635 . . . 7-D6
Grand Prairie 71,462 . . . 9-B8,25-D5
Grand Saline 2,709 . . . 11-C5
Grandview 1,205 . . . 9-C8
Granger . . . 15-A8
Granger 1,236 . . . 17-B6
Grapeland 1,634 . . . 11-D5
Grapevine 11,801 . . . 9-B8,24-B4
Grassland . . . 8-A2
Grayburg 194 . . . 17-B7
Green Lake . . . 16-D4
Greenville • 22,161 . . . 10-B4
Greenvine . . . 16-B4
Greenwood . . . 9-A7
Gregory 2,739 . . . 19-A6
Grey Forest . . . 29-B5
Grigsby . . . 11-D7
Grit . . . 15-A5
Groesbeck • 3,373 . . . 10-D4
Groom 736 . . . 4-B4
Grosvenor . . . 9-C5
Grove, The . . . 9-D7
Groves 17,090 . . . 17-B8
Groveton • 1,262 . . . 17-A6
Gruver 1,216 . . . 4-A4
Guerra . . . 18-C4
Gunter 849 . . . 10-A3
Gustine 416 . . . 9-C6
Guthrie • . . . 8-A4
Guy . . . 17-C5
Hagansport . . . 11-B6
Hainesville . . . 11-B5
Hale Center 2,297 . . . 4-D3
Hallettsville • 2,865 . . . 16-C3
Hallsville 1,556 . . . 11-C6
Haltom City 29,014 . . . 24-C2
Hamby . . . 9-B5
Hamilton • 3,189 . . . 9-C7
Hamlin 3,248 . . . 8-B4
Hammond . . . 16-A4
Hamshire . . . 17-B7
Happy 674 . . . 4-C3
Happy Valley . . . 8-C4
Hardin 719 . . . 17-B6
Hargill . . . 19-C5
Harker Heights 7,345 . . . 9-D7
Harleton . . . 11-B7
Harlingen 43,543 . . . 19-D6
Harper . . . 15-B5
Harriett . . . 8-D4
Harrold . . . 5-D7
Hart 1,008 . . . 4-C3
Hart Camp . . . 4-D3
Hartley . . . 4-A3
Harvey . . . 16-A4
Harwood . . . 15-C8
Haskell • 3,782 . . . 8-A4
Haslet . . . 9-B8,24-B2
Hastings . . . 26-F3
Hatchel . . . 8-C4
Hawkins 1,302 . . . 11-C5
Hawley 679 . . . 8-B4
Haynesville . . . 5-D8
Hazel . . . 4-C3
Hearne 5,418 . . . 16-A4
Hebbronville • . . . 18-B4
Hebron . . . 25-A6
Hedley 380 . . . 5-C5
Hedwig Village 2,506 . . . 26-C1
Hefner . . . 9-A5
Heidenheimer . . . 9-D8
Helena . . . 15-D8
Helotes . . . 15-C6,29-B5
Hemphill • 1,353 . . . 11-D8
Hempstead • 3,456 . . . 17-B5
Henderson • 11,473 . . . 11-C6
Henrietta • 3,149 . . . 10-A1
Hereford • 15,853 . . . 4-C2
Hermleigh . . . 8-B3
Herty . . . 11-D7
Hewitt . . . 9-D8
Hext . . . 9-D5
Hicks . . . 24-B1
Hico 1,375 . . . 9-C7
Hidalgo 2,288 . . . 19-D5
Higgins 702 . . . 5-A6
High Island . . . 17-C7
Highland Park . . . 25-C7
Highlands . . . 17-B6
Hightower . . . 17-B6
Hill Country Village . . . 29-B6
Hillister . . . 17-A7
Hillje . . . 16-C4
Hillsboro • 7,397 . . . 9-C8
Hilltop Lakes . . . 16-A4
Hilshire Village . . . 26-C1
Hindes . . . 15-D6
Hitchcock 6,655 . . . 17-C6,27-E6
Hobson . . . 15-D7
Hochheim . . . 15-C8
Hockley . . . 17-B5
Hodges . . . 8-B4
Holland 863 . . . 9-D8
Holliday 1,349 . . . 5-D8
Holly . . . 17-A5
Holly Springs . . . 17-A8
Hollywood Park . . . 29-B6
Hondo • 6,057 . . . 15-C5
Honey Grove 1,973 . . . 11-A5
Hood . . . 9-A8
Hooks 2,507 . . . 11-A7
Hoover . . . 5-B5
Horizon City . . . 6-C2
Hot Wells . . . 6-D3
Houston • 1,594,086 . . . 17-B5,26-D2
Howe 2,072 . . . 10-A3
Howland . . . 11-A5
Hubbard 1,676 . . . 10-D3
Huckabay . . . 9-B6
Hueco . . . 6-C2
Hufsmith . . . 17-B5
Hughes Springs 2,196 . . . 11-B6
Hull . . . 17-B7
Humble 6,729 . . . 17-B6,26-A3
Hungerford . . . 17-C5
Hunt . . . 15-B5
Hunter . . . 15-C7
Huntington 1,672 . . . 11-D7
Hunters Creek Village . . . 26-C1
Hunton . . . 5-A5
Huntsville • 23,936 . . . 17-A5
Hurlwood . . . 7-A8
Huron . . . 9-C8
Hurst 31,420 . . . 24-C3
Hurstown . . . 11-D7
Hutchins 2,996 . . . 25-E8
Hutto 659 . . . 15-B8
Huxley . . . 11-D8
Hye . . . 15-B6
Iago . . . 17-C5
Idalou 2,348 . . . 4-D4
Illinois Bend . . . 10-A2
Imperial . . . 7-D7
Inadale . . . 8-B3
Independence . . . 16-B4
Indian Creek . . . 9-C5
Indian Gap . . . 9-C6
Indianola . . . 16-D4
Industry . . . 16-B4
Inez . . . 16-D4
Ingleside 5,436 . . . 19-A6
Ingram . . . 15-B5
Iola . . . 17-A5
Iowa Park 6,184 . . . 5-D8
Ira . . . 8-B3
Iraan 1,358 . . . 7-D8
Iredell 407 . . . 9-C7
Ireland . . . 9-C7
Irene . . . 10-C3
Irving 109,943 . . . 10-B3,25-C5
Island . . . 17-A5
Italy 1,306 . . . 10-C3
Itasca 1,600 . . . 9-C8
Ivan . . . 9-B6
Ivanhoe . . . 10-A4
Izoro . . . 9-D7
Jacinto City 8,953 . . . 26-C3
Jacksboro • 4,000 . . . 9-A6
Jacksonville 12,264 . . . 11-C5
James . . . 11-D7
Jarrell . . . 15-A8
Jasper • 6,959 . . . 17-A7
Jayton • 638 . . . 8-A3
Jean . . . 9-A6
Jefferson • 2,643 . . . 11-B7
Jermyn . . . 9-A6
Jersey Village . . . 26-B1
Jewett 597 . . . 10-D4
Joaquin 917 . . . 11-C7
Johnson . . . 7-A7
Johnson City • 872 . . . 15-B7
Johntown . . . 11-A6
Jolly . . . 10-A1

Place Population	Page Grid
Alvin 16,515	17-C6

Jollyville	15-B7
Jonah	15-B8
Jonesboro	9-C7
Jones Creek 2,634	17-D6
Jonestown	22-B1
Jonesville	11-C7
Joplin	9-A7
Josephine 416	10-B4
Joshua 1,470	9-B8
Jourdanton • 2,743	15-D6
Judson	11-C6
Junction • 2,593	14-B4
Juno	14-B2
Justiceburg	8-A2
Justin 920	9-A8
Kalgary	8-A2
Kamay	5-D8
Karnack	11-B7
Karnes City • 3,296	15-D7
Katemcy	9-D5
Katy 5,660	17-C5
Kaufman • 4,658	10-C4
Keene 3,013	9-B8
Keller 4,143	9-B8,24-B3
Kellevrille	5-B5
Kelseybass	19-C5
Kelton	5-B6
Kemah 1,304	27-C6
Kemp 1,035	10-C4
Kempner	9-D7
Kendalia	15-C6
Kendleton	17-C5
Kenedy 4,356	15-D7
Kennard 424	11-D6
Kennedale 2,594	9-B8,24-E3
Kenney	16-B4
Kent	7-D5
Kerens 1,582	10-C4
Kermit • 8,015	7-C6
Kerrick	4-A3
Kerrville • 15,276	15-B5
Key	7-B8
Kildare Junction	11-B7
Kilgore 10,968	11-C6
Killeen 46,296	9-D7
King	9-D7
Kingsbury	15-C7
Kingsland	15-B6
Kingsmill	5-B5
Kingston	10-B4
Kingsville • 28,808	19-B6
Kingwood	17-B6
Kinwood	26-B3
Kirby	29-C7
Kirbyville 1,972	17-A7
Kirkland	5-D6
Kirvin	10-D4
Knickerbocker	8-D3
Knippa	15-C5
Knott	8-B2
Knox City 1,546	8-A4
Koockville	15-A5
Kopperl	9-C8
Kosciusko	15-D7
Kosse 484	10-D4
Koutze • 2,716	17-B7
Kress 783	4-D3
Krum 917	9-A8
Kurten	16-A4
Kyle 2,093	15-B7
La Blanca	19-D5
La Casa	9-B6
Lacoste 862	15-C6
Lacy-Lakeview 2,752	9-C8
Ladonia 761	10-A4
La Feria 3,495	19-D6
Lagarto	19-C5
La Gloria	19-C5
La Grange • 3,768	16-B3
La Grulla 1,442	18-D4
Laguna	14-C4
La Isla	6-C2
La Joya 2,018	19-D5
Lake Creek	11-A5
Lake Dallas 3,177	9-A8
Lakehills	15-C6
Lake Jackson 19,102	17-C6
Lakeside	24-C1
Lakeside	28-F3
Laketon	5-B5
Lakeview	5-C5
Lakeview	7-A8
Lakeway 790	15-B7,22-C1
Lake Worth	24-C1
Lamar	19-A7
La Marque 15,372	17-C6,27-E6
Lamesa • 11,790	7-B8
Lamkin	9-C7
Lampasas • 6,165	9-D6
Lancaster 14,807	10-C3,25-F7
Lane City	17-C5
Laneville	11-C6
Langtry	13-C7
Lanier	11-B7
La Paloma	19-D6
La Porte 14,062	17-C6,27-B6
La Pryor	14-D4
Laredo • 91,449	18-B3
Lariat	4-D2
Lark	4-B4
La Rue	11-C5
La Salle	16-D4
Lasara	19-C5
Lassater	11-B7
Latexo	11-D5
La Vernia 632	15-C7,29-D8
La Villa 1,442	19-D5
Lavon	10-B4
La Ward	16-D4
Lawn 390	8-C4
Lazbuddie	4-D2
Leaday	9-C5
League City 16,598	17-C6,27-D5
Leagueville	11-C5
Leakey • 468	14-C4
Leander 2,179	15-B7,22-A2
Ledbetter	16-B3
Leesburg	11-B6
Leesville	15-C7
Lefors 829	5-B5
Leggett	17-A6
Lehman	7-A7
Leigh	11-C7
Lela	5-B6
Lelia Lake	5-C5
Leming	15-D6,29-F6
Leona 165	17-A5
Leonard 1,421	10-B4
Leon Springs	15-C6,29-B5
Leon Valley	29-C5
Leroy	9-C8
Lesley	5-C5
Levelland • 13,809	7-A7
Levita	9-D7
Lewisville 24,273	9-A8,25-A5
Lexington 1,065	16-B3
Liberty • 7,945	17-B6
Liberty Hill	15-B7
Lincoln	16-B3
Lindale 2,180	11-C5
Linden • 2,443	11-B7
Lingleville	9-C6
Linn	19-C5
Linwood	11-D6
Lipan 435	9-B7
Lipscomb •	5-A6
Lissie	16-C4
Little Elm	9-A8
Littlefield • 7,409	4-D2
Little River-Academy 1,155	9-D8
Live Oak	29-C7
Livingston • 4,928	17-A6
Llano • 3,071	15-A6
Lockett	5-D7
Lockhart 7,913	15-C8
Lockney 2,334	4-D4
Lodi	11-B7
Logan	11-C7
Logansport	11-C7
Lohn	9-D5
Lolita	16-D4
Loma Alta	14-C3
Lometa 666	9-D6
London	15-B5
Lone Camp	9-B7
Lone Grove	9-D6
Lone Oak 467	11-B5,29-D8
Lone Star 2,036	11-B6
Long Lake	11-D5
Long Mott	16-D4
Longview • 62,762	11-C6
Longworth	8-B4
Loop	7-B7
Lopeno	18-C4
Loraine 929	8-B3
Lorena 619	9-D8
Lorenzo 1,394	8-A2
Los Angeles	18-A4
Los Fresnos 2,173	19-D6
Lott 865	16-A3
Louise	16-D4
Lovelady 509	17-A5
Loving	9-A6
Lowake	8-D4
Loyal Valley	15-B6
Loyola Beach	19-B6
Lubbock • 173,979	8-A2,28-C2
Lucas	10-B4
Luckenbach	15-B6
Lueders 420	9-B5
Lufkin • 28,562	11-D6
Luling 5,039	15-C8
Lumberton	17-B7
Luther	8-B2
Lutie	5-C6
Lydia	11-A6
Lyford 1,618	19-C6
Lyons	16-B4
Lytle 1,920	15-C6
Mabank 1,443	10-C4
Mabelle	5-D7
Macdona	29-D5
Mackay	16-C4
Madisonville • 3,660	17-A5
Magnet	17-C5
Magnolia 867	17-B5
Magnolia Beach	16-D4
Magnolia Springs	17-A7
Malakoff 2,082	10-C4
Malone 315	10-D3
Malta	11-A6
Malvern	11-D5
Manchaca	22-F2
Manchester	11-A6
Manheim	16-B3
Mankins	5-D8
Manor 1,044	15-B8
Mansfield 8,092	9-B8,24-F4
Manvel	17-C6
Maple	4-D2
Marathon	13-C6
Marble Falls 3,252	15-B7
Marco	9-D5
Marfa • 2,466	12-C4
Margaret	5-D7
Marietta 169	11-B7
Marion	15-C7,29-B8
Markham	17-D5
Markley	9-A6
Marlin • 7,099	10-D3
Marquez 231	16-A4
Marshall • 24,921	11-C7
Mart 2,324	10-D3
Martindale	15-C7
Martinsville	11-D7
Maryette	9-A7
Maryneal	8-C3
Marysville	10-A2
Mason • 2,153	15-A5
Masterson	4-B3
Matador • 1,052	5-D5
Matagorda	17-D5
Mathias 5,667	19-A6
Maud 1,059	11-B7
Mauriceville	17-B8
Maverick	8-C4
May	9-C6
Maydelle	11-D5
Mayflower	17-A8
Maypearl 626	9-B8
Maysfield	16-A3
McAdoo	5-D5
McAllen 67,042	19-D5
McCamey 2,436	7-D8
McCaulley	8-B4
McCook	19-C5
McCoy	15-D7
McFaddin	16-D3
McGregor 4,513	9-D8
McKinney • 16,249	10-B3
McLean 1,160	5-B5
McLeod	11-B7
McMahan	15-C8
McNary	6-D2
McQueeney	15-C7
Meadow 591	7-A8
Medina	15-C5
Megargel 381	9-A6
Melissa 604	10-B4
Melrose	11-D7
Melvin 202	9-D5
Memphis • 3,352	5-C5
Menard • 1,697	8-D4
Mentone •	7-C6
Mercedes 11,851	19-D5
Mercers Gap	9-C6
Mercury	9-D5
Mereta	8-D4
Meridian • 1,330	9-C8
Merkel 2,493	8-B4
Mertens	10-C3
Mertzon • 687	8-D3
Mesquite 67,053	10-B3,25-D8
Mexia 7,094	10-D4
Meyersville	15-D8
Miami • 813	5-B5
Mico	15-C6
Midfield	16-D4
Midkiff	7-C8
Midland • 70,525	7-C7,28-B3
Midlothian 3,219	10-C3
Midway	17-A5,29-E5
Milam	11-D8
Milano 468	16-A3
Miles 720	8-C4
Miller Grove	11-B5
Millersview	8-D4
Millett	15-D5
Millford 681	10-C3
Millican	16-B4
Millsap 439	9-B7
Mineola 4,346	11-C5
Mineral	15-D7
Mineral Wells 14,468	9-B6
Mingus 212	9-B6
Minter	11-A5
Mirando City	18-B4
Mission 22,589	19-D5
Mission Valley	16-D3
Missouri City	26-E1
Mobeetie 291	5-B5
Moline	9-D7
Moahans • 8,937	7-C7
Monkstown	10-A4
Monroe	11-C6
Monroe City	17-B7
Montague •	9-A7
Montalba	11-D5
Mont Belvieu 1,730	17-B6
Monte Alto	19-C5
Montel	14-C4
Montgomery 258	17-B5
Moody 1,385	9-D8
Moore	15-D6
Moores Crossing	22-F4
Moran 344	9-B5
Morgan 485	9-C8
Morgan Mill	9-B7
Morgan's Point	9-D8,27-B6
Morse	4-A4
Morton • 2,674	4-D2
Morton Valley	9-B6
Moscow	17-A6
Mosheim	9-C7
Mosses Hill	17-B7
Moulton 1,009	16-C3
Mountain Home	15-B5
Mount Blanco	4-D4
Mount Calm 393	10-D3
Mount Enterprise 485	11-C7
Mount Pleasant • 11,003	11-B6
Mount Selman	11-C6
Mount Sylvan	11-C5
Mount Vernon • 2,025	11-B6
Muenster 1,408	9-A8
Muleshoe • 4,842	4-D2
Mullin 213	9-D6
Mumford	16-A4
Munday 1,738	9-A5
Murchison	11-C5
Murphy	25-A8
Murray	9-A6
Myrtle Springs	10-C4
Nacogdoches • 27,149	11-D6
Nada	16-C4
Nameless	22-B1
Naples 1,908	11-B6
Nash 2,022	11-A7
Nassau Bay	17-C6,27-C5
Natalia 1,264	15-D6
Navasota 5,971	17-B5
Nazareth	4-C3
Neches	11-D5
Nederland 16,855	17-B7
Needmore	4-D2
Needville 1,417	17-C5
Negley	11-A6
Neinda	8-B4
Nelsonville	16-B4
Nemo	9-C7
Newark	24-A1
New Baden	16-A4
New Berlin	15-C7
New Boston 4,628	11-A7
New Braunsfels • 22,402	15-C7
Newburg	9-C6
New Caney	17-B6
Newcastle 688	9-A6
New Deal	4-D3
Newgulf	17-C5
New Home	7-A8
Newlin	5-C5
New London 942	11-C6
Newlynn	8-A2
New Moore	7-B8
Newport	9-A7
New Salem	11-C6
Newsome	11-B6
New Summerfield 319	11-C6
New Taiton	16-C4
Newton • 1,620	17-A8
New Ulm	16-B4
New Waverly 824	17-B5
New Willard	17-A6
Nickle Creek	6-C4
Nimrod	9-C5
Nixon 2,008	15-C8
Nocona 2,992	10-A2
Nolan	8-C4
Nolanville	9-D8
Noodle	8-B4
Noonday	11-C5
Nordheim 369	15-D8
Normandy	14-D3
Normangee 636	16-A4
Normanna	15-D7
North	17-B6
North Cowden	7-C7
Northfield	5-D5
North Houston	26-B1
Northlake	24-A2
North Richland Hills	24-C3
North Zulch	16-A4
Norton	8-C4
Notrees	7-C7
Novice	11-A5
Novice	9-C5
Nubia	8-B4
Nugent	9-B5
Nursery	16-D3
Oakalla	9-D7
Oak Grove	24-F2
Oak Grove	11-A6
Oak Hill	22-E2
Oakhurst	17-A6
Oak Island	17-C6
Oak Ridge	17-B6
Oakville	19-A5
Oakwood 606	11-D5
Oatmeal	15-B7
O,Brien 212	8-A4
Odds	10-D4
Odell	5-D7
Odem 2,363	19-A6
Odessa • 90,027	7-C8,28-E1
O,Donnell 1,200	7-B8
Oglesby 470	9-D8
Oilton	18-B4
Oklaunion	5-D7
Okra	9-C6
Old Dime Box	16-B3
Olden	9-B6
Oldenburg	16-B4
Old Glory	8-A4
Old Odean	17-D5
Oletha	10-D4
Olin	9-C7
Olivia	16-D4
Olmito	19-D6
Olmos Park 2,069	15-C6,29-C6
Olney 4,060	9-A6
Olton 2,235	4-D3
Omaha 960	11-B6
Onalaska	17-A6
Opdyke West	7-A8
Oplin	9-C5
Orange • 23,628	17-B8
Orange Grove 1,212	19-A5
Ore City 1,050	11-B6
Orla	7-C5
Osage	9-D7
Osceola	9-C8
Ovalo	8-C4
Overton 2,430	11-C6
Ovilla	25-F6
Owens	8-A2
Owens	9-C6
Owenton	11-C6
Oxford	15-B6
Ozona •	14-A2
Padgett	9-A6
Paducah • 2,216	5-D5
Paige	16-B3
Paint Rock • 256	8-D4
Palacios 4,667	16-D4
Palestine • 15,948	11-D5
Palito Blanco	19-B5
Palmer 1,187	10-C3
Paloduro	4-C4
Palo Pinto •	9-B7
Paluxy	9-C7
Pampa • 21,396	5-B5
Pandale	13-C7
Pandora	15-C7
Panhandle • 2,226	4-B4
Pantego	24-D3
Panther Junction	13-D6
Papalote	19-A6
Paris • 25,498	11-A5
Parker 1,098	9-C8,25-A8
Park Springs	9-A7
Pasadena 112,560	17-C6,26-D4
Patricia	7-B8
Patroon	11-D8
Pattison 318	17-B5
Pattonville	11-A5
Pawnee	15-D7
Paxton	11-C7
Payne Springs	10-C4
Peacock	8-A4
Pearl	9-D7
Pearland 13,248	17-C6,26-F3
Pearsall • 7,383	15-D6
Pear Valley	9-D5
Peaster	9-B7
Pecan Gap 250	11-A5
Pecos • 12,855	7-D6
Peeltown	10-C4
Peerless	11-B5
Penelope	10-D3
Pennington	17-A5
Penwell	7-C7
Peoria	9-C8
Pep	4-D2
Percilla	11-D5
Perico	4-A2
Perrin	9-B7
Perry	10-D3
Perryton • 7,991	5-A5
Perryville	11-B5
Persimmon Gap Ranger Station	13-C5
Peters	16-B4
Petersburg 1,633	4-D4
Petit	4-D2
Petrolia	10-A1
Petronilla	19-B6
Pettit	15-D7
Pflugerville	15-B8,22-C4
Pharr 21,381	19-D5
Phillips	4-B4
Pickton	11-B5
Pidcoke	9-D7
Pierce	16-C4
Pilot Knob	22-F3
Pilot Point 2,211	10-B3
Pinehurst	17-B5
Pineland 1,111	11-D7
Pine Mills	11-B6
Pine Springs	6-C4
Piney Point Village	26-C1
Pioneer	9-C5
Pipecreek	15-C6
Pittsburg • 4,245	11-B6
Placedo	16-D4
Placid	9-D5
Plains • 1,457	7-A7
Plainview • 22,187	4-D3
Plano 72,331	10-B3,25-A7
Plantersville	17-B5
Plaska	5-C5
Pleasanton 6,346	15-D6
Pleasant Valley	28-D3
Pledger	17-C5
Plemons	4-B4
Plum	16-B3
Point 468	11-B5
Point Blank	17-A6
Point Comfort 1,125	16-D4
Pollok	11-D5
Ponder 297	9-A8
Ponta	11-D6
Pontotoc	9-D5
Poolville	9-B7
Porfirio	19-C6
Port Acres	17-B8
Port Aransas 1,968	19-A7
Port Arthur 61,195	17-B8
Port Bolivar	17-C7,27-E8
Porter	17-B6
Port Isabel 3,769	19-D6
Portland 12,023	19-A6,23-D6
Port Lavaca • 10,911	16-D4
Port Mansfield	19-C6
Port Neches	17-B8
Port O'Connor	16-D4
Posey	8-A2
Post • 3,961	8-A2
Postoak	9-A7
Poteet 3,086	15-D6
Poth 1,461	15-D7
Pottsboro 895	10-A3
Pottsville	9-C6
Powderly	11-A5
Powell	10-C4
Poynor	11-C5
Prairie Hill	10-D3
Prairie Lea	15-C7
Prairie View 3,993	17-B5
Premont 2,984	19-B5
Presidio	12-D4
Price	11-C6
Priddy	9-C6
Princeton 3,408	10-B4
Pringle	4-A4
Pritchett	11-B6
Proffitt	9-A5
Progreso	19-D5
Progress	4-D2
Prosper 675	10-B3
Puerto Rico	19-C5
Pumpville	13-C7
Purdon	10-D4
Purley	11-B5
Purmela	9-D7
Purves	9-C7
Putnam	9-B5
Pyote 382	7-C6
Quanah • 3,890	5-D6
Queen City 1,748	11-B7
Quemado	14-D3
Quinlan 1,002	10-B4
Quitaque 696	5-D5
Quitman • 1,893	11-B5
Rachal	19-C5
Radium	8-B4
Raisin	16-D3
Ralls 2,422	4-D4
Ramirito	18-C4
Rampa	5-B5
Randado	18-C4
Randolph	10-A4
Ranger 3,142	9-B6
Rankin • 1,216	7-D8
Ratcliff	11-D6
Rayburn	17-B6
Raymondville • 9,493	19-C5
Raywood	17-B7
Reagan	16-A3
Reagan Wells	14-C4
Realitos	18-B4
Redford	12-D4
Red Hill	11-B7
Redland	11-D5
Red Oak 1,882	10-C3
Red Rock	15-B8
Red Springs	9-A5
Redwater	11-A7
Reese	11-C5
Refugio • 3,898	19-A6
Reklaw	11-D6
Rendon	24-F3
Reno 1,059	11-A5
Retta	24-F3
Rhineland	9-A5
Rhome 478	9-A8
Rhonesboro	11-B6
Ricardo	19-B5
Rice 439	10-C4
Richards 260	17-B5
Richardson 72,496	24-A1,25-B7
Richland 260	10-D4
Richland Hills	24-C3
Richland Springs 420	9-D6
Richmond • 9,692	17-C5
Richwood 2,591	17-D6
Ridge	16-A4
Ridgeway	11-B5
Riesel 691	10-D3
Ringgold	10-A2
Rio Grande City •	18-C4
Rio Grande Village Ranger Station	13-D6
Rio Hondo 1,673	19-D6
Riomedina	15-C6
Rio Vista	9-C8
Rising Star 1,204	9-C5
River Oaks	24-D1
Riverland	10-A1
Riverside 425	17-A6
Riviera	19-B5
Riviera Beach	19-B6
Roanoke 910	9-B8,24-A3
Roans Prairie	17-A5
Roaring Springs 315	5-D5
Robert Lee • 1,202	8-C3
Robertson	8-A2
Robinson 6,074	9-D8
Robstown 12,100	19-A6
Roby • 814	8-B3
Rochell	9-D5
Rochester 492	8-A4
Rockdale 5,611	16-A3
Rock Island	16-C4
Rockland	17-A7
Rockne	15-B8
Rockport • 3,686	19-A7
Rocksprings • 1,317	14-B4
Rockwall • 5,939	10-B4
Rockwood	9-D5
Rocky Ranch	11-B6
Rogers 1,242	9-D8
Roland	10-A2
Rollingwood	22-E2
Roma-Los Saenz 3,384	18-C4
Romney	9-C6
Roosevelt	14-B4
Ropesville 489	7-A8
Rosanky	15-C8
Roscoe 1,628	8-B3
Rosebud 2,076	16-A3
Rosenberg 17,995	17-C5
Rosewood	11-B6
Rosharon	17-C6
Ross City	8-C2
Rosser	10-C4
Rotan 2,284	8-B3
Round Mountain	15-B6
Round Rock 11,812	15-B8,22-A3
Round Top	16-B3
Rowden	9-C5
Rowena	8-C4
Roxton	11-A5
Roy	4-C3
Royalty	7-D7
Royse City 1,566	10-B4
Royston	8-B3
Rucker	9-C6
Ruidosa	12-C3
Rule 1,015	8-A4
Runge 1,244	15-D8
Rusk • 4,681	11-D6
Russeltown	19-D6
Rutersville	16-B3
Rye	17-B7
Sabinal 1,827	15-C5
Sabine	17-B8
Sabine Pass	17-B8
Sachse	25-A8
Sacul	11-D6
Sagerton	8-A4
Saginaw 5,736	9-B8,24-C2
St. Francis	4-B4
St. Hedwig	29-D8
St. Jo 1,071	9-A8
St. Paul	19-A6
Salado	9-D8
Salesville	9-B7
Salineno	18-C4
Salmon	11-D5
Salt Flat	6-C3
Saltillo	11-B5
Samnorwood	5-C6
San Angelo • 73,240	8-C3
San Antonio • 785,410	15-C6,29-D6
San Augustine • 2,930	11-D7
San Benito 17,988	19-D6
Sanco	8-C3
Sanderson •	13-C7
Sandia	19-A5
San Diego • 5,225	19-B5
Sand Ridge	17-A5
Sandsprings	8-C2
Sandy	15-B6
Sandy Point	17-C5
San Elizaria	6-C2
San Felipe 532	17-C5
Sanford 249	4-B4
San Gabriel	15-A8
Sanger 2,574	9-A8
San Isidro	19-C5
San Juan 7,608	19-D5
San Leanna	22-F2
San Leon	17-C6,27-D7
San Marcos • 23,420	15-C7
San Patricio	19-A6
San Perlita 475	19-C6
San Saba • 2,366	9-D6
Sansom Park Village 3,921	24-C1
Santa Ana 1,535	9-C5
Santa Catarina	18-C4
Santa Fe 5,413	17-C6,27-E5
Santa Maria	19-D6
Santa Rita	8-D2
Santa Rosa 1,889	19-D5
Santo	9-B7
San Ygnacio	18-C3
Saragosa	7-D6
Saratoga	17-B7
Sargent	17-D5
Sarita •	19-B6
Sattler	15-C7
Savoy 855	10-A4
Sayers	15-C7,29-D7
Schattel	15-D6
Schertz 7,262	15-C7,29-C8
Schulenburg 2,469	16-C3
Schwab City	17-A6
Schwertner	15-A8
Scotland 367	9-A6
Scranton	9-B5
Scroggins	11-B5
Scurry	10-C4
Seabrook 4,670	17-C6,27-C6
Seadrift 1,277	19-A7
Seagoville 7,304	10-C4
Seagraves 2,596	7-B7
Sealy 3,875	16-C4
Sebastian	19-C5
Segno	17-A7
Seguin • 17,854	15-C7
Selfs	10-A4
Selma	29-B7
Selman City	11-C6
Seminole • 6,080	7-B7
Senate	9-A6
Seven Pines	11-C6
Seymour • 3,657	9-A5
Shafter	12-C4
Shallowater 1,932	4-D3
Shamrock 2,834	5-B6
Shannon	9-A6
Shavano Park	29-B6
Sheffield	13-B8
Shields	9-C5
Shelbyville	11-D7
Sheldon	17-B6
Shepherd 1,674	17-B6
Sheridan	16-C4
Sherman • 30,413	10-A3
Shiner 2,213	15-C8
Shiro	17-A5
Shoreacres	27-B6
Sidney	9-C6
Sierra Blanca •	6-D3
Silsbee 7,684	17-B7
Silver	8-C3
Silver City	10-C4
Silverton • 918	4-C4
Silver Valley	9-C5
Simmons	19-A5
Simms	11-B6
Singleton	17-A5
Sinton • 6,044	19-A6
Sipe Springs	9-C6
Sisterdale	15-B6
Sivells Bend	10-A3
Skellytown 899	4-B4
Skidmore	19-A6
Slaton 6,804	8-A2
Slidell	9-A8
Slocum	11-D5
Smiley 439	15-C8
Smithland	11-B7
Smith Point	17-C7,27-C8
Smithville 3,470	16-B3
Smithwick	15-B7
Smyer	7-A8
Snook	16-B4
Snyder • 12,705	8-B3
Socorro	6-C2
Soda	17-A6
Solino	19-C5
Somerset 1,102	15-C6,29-E5
Somerville 1,814	16-B4
Sonora • 3,856	14-B3
Sour Lake 1,807	17-B7
South Bend	9-B6
South Houston 13,293	17-C6,26-D4
Southlake	24-B3
Southland	8-A2
Southmayd	10-A3
South Padre Island	19-D7
South Plains	4-D4
Southside Place	26-D2
Spade	4-D3
Spanish Fort	10-A2
Speaks	16-C4
Spearman • 3,413	4-A4
Splendora	17-B6
Spofford	14-D3
Spring	17-B6
Spring Creek	9-A5
Springlake 222	4-D3
Springtown 1,658	9-B7
Spring Valley 3,353	26-C1
Sprinkle	22-D4
Spur 1,690	8-A3
Spurger	17-A7
Stacy	9-D5
Stafford 4,755	17-C5,26-E1
Stamford 4,542	8-B4
Stanton • 2,314	7-C8
Staples	15-C7
Star	9-D7
Stephenville • 11,881	9-C6
Sterley	4-D4
Sterling City • 915	8-C3
Stiles	8-D2
Stinnett • 2,222	4-B4
Stith	8-B4
Stockdale 1,265	15-C7
Stoneburg	9-A7
Stoneham	17-B5
Stonewall	15-B6
Stowell	17-C7
Stratford • 1,917	4-A3
Strawn 694	9-B6
Streeter	15-A5
Streetman 415	10-D4
Structure	15-B8
Study Butte	13-D5
Sublime	16-C3
Sudan 1,091	4-D2
Sugar Land 8,826	17-C5
Sullivan City	18-D4
Sulphur Bluff	11-B5
Sulphur Springs • 12,804	11-B5
Summerfield	4-C3
Sundown 1,511	7-A7
Suniland 1,952	15-D7
Sunray 1,952	4-A4
Sunrise	16-A3
Sunset	9-A7
Sunset Valley	22-E2
Sutherland Springs	15-C7
Swan	11-C5
Swearingen	5-D6
Sweeney 3,538	17-D5
Sweet Home	16-C3
Sweetwater • 12,242	8-B4
Swenson	8-A3
Sylvester	8-B4
Tadmor	11-D6
Taft 3,686	19-A6
Tahoka • 3,262	7-A8
Talco 751	11-B6
Talpa	9-C5
Tamina	17-B6
Tanglewood	16-B3
Tankersley	8-D3
Tarpley	15-C5
Tascosa	4-B3
Tatum 1,339	11-C7
Taylor 10,619	15-B8
Taylor Lake Village	27-C6
Teacup	15-B5
Teague 3,390	10-D4
Tehuacana 265	10-D4
Telegraph	14-B4
Telephone	10-A4
Tell	5-D5
Temple 42,483	9-D8
Tenaha 1,005	11-C7
Tennessee Colony	11-D5
Tennyson	8-C3
Terlingua	13-D5
Terrell 13,225	10-B4
Terrell Hills 4,644	15-C7,29-C6
Texahoma	4-A3
Texarkana 31,271	11-A7
Texas City 41,403	17-C6,27-E7
Texline 477	4-A2
Texon	8-D2
Thalia	5-D7
Thelma	29-E6
Thomas	11-B6
Thomaston	15-D8
Thompsonville	15-C8
Thornberry	10-A1
Thorndale 1,300	15-B8
Thornton 498	10-D4
Thorp Spring	9-B7
Thrall 573	15-B8
Three Points	22-C4
Three Rivers 2,133	15-D7
Throckmorton • 1,174	9-A5
Tilden •	18-A4
Timpson 1,164	11-C7
Tin Top	9-B7
Tioga 511	10-B3
Tivoli	16-D3
Tokio	7-A7
Tolar 415	9-B7
Tolbert	5-D7
Tolosa	10-C4
Tomball 3,996	17-B5
Tom Bean	10-A4
Topsey	9-D7
Tornillo	6-C2
Tow	9-D6
Town Bluff	17-A7
Toyah 165	7-D5
Toyahvale	7-D5
Travis	16-A3
Trawick	11-D6
Trebor	11-B6
Trent 313	8-B4
Trenton 691	10-B4
Trickham	9-C5
Trinidad 1,130	10-C4
Trinity 2,452	17-A5
Troup 1,911	11-C6
Troy 1,353	9-D8
Truby	8-B4
Truscott	5-D6
Tucker	11-D5
Tuleta	15-D8
Tulia • 5,033	4-C3
Tunis	16-D4
Turkey 644	5-C5
Turlington	10-D4
Turnersville	9-C7
Tuscola 660	8-C4
Tuxedo	8-B4
Twin Sisters	15-B6
Twichell	5-A5
Twitty	5-B6
Tye	8-B4
Tyler • 70,508	11-C6
Tynan	19-A6
Umbarger	4-C3
Uncertain	11-B7
Unity	11-A5
Universal City 10,720	15-C6,29-C7
University Park 22,254	10-B3,25-C7
Urbana	17-A6
Utopia	15-C5
Uvalde • 14,178	14-D4
Valentine 328	12-B4
Valera	9-C5
Valley Mills 1,236	9-C8
Valley Spring	9-D6
Valley View 514	9-A8
Valley Wells	18-A3
Van 1,881	11-C5
Van Alystyne 1,860	10-B3
Vancourt	8-D4
Vanderbilt	16-D4
Vanderpool	15-C5
Van Horn • 2,772	6-D4
Van Vleck	17-D5
Vashti	9-A7
Vega • 900	4-B2
Venus 518	9-B8
Vera	9-A5
Verhalen	7-D6
Veribest	8-D4
Vernon • 12,695	5-D7
Viboras	18-C4
Victoria • 50,695	16-D3
Vidaurri	16-D3
Vidor 12,117	17-B7
Vienna	16-C4
View	8-B4
Vigo Park	4-C4
Village Mills	17-A7
Vincent	8-B2
Voca	9-D5
Volente	22-C1
Von Ormy	15-C6,29-E5
Voss	9-C5
Votaw	17-B7
Waco • 101,261	9-C8
Wadsworth	17-D5
Waelder 942	15-C8
Waka	5-A5
Walburg	15-A8
Wall	8-D4
Waller 1,241	17-B5
Wallis 1,138	17-C5
Walnut Springs 613	9-C7
Warda	16-B3
Ware	4-A2
Warren 281	17-A7
Warrenton	16-B3
Washburn	4-B4
Washington	16-B4
Waskom 1,821	11-C7
Wastella	8-B3
Watagua 10,284	24-C3
Water Valley	8-C3
Watson	9-D7
Waxahachie • 14,624	10-C3
Wayside	4-C4
Weatherford • 12,049	9-B7
Weatherly	5-C5
Weaver	11-B5
Webb	18-B3
Webster 2,168	27-C5
Weches	11-D6
Weesatche	15-D8
Weimar 2,096	16-C3
Weinert 253	9-A5
Welch	7-B8
Welcome	16-B4
Wellborn	16-B4
Wellington • 3,043	5-C5
Wellman	7-B7
Wells 926	11-D6
Weser	15-D8
Weslaco 19,331	19-D5
West 2,485	9-C8
Westbrook	8-B2
West Columbia 4,109	17-C5
Westoff	15-D8
Westlake	24-A3
West Lake Hills	22-D2
Westminster	10-B4
Weston 405	10-B3
Westover	9-A5
Westover Hills	24-D1
West Point	16-B3
West Point	7-A8
West University Place 12,010	26-D2
Westworth 3,651	24-D1
Wharton • 9,033	17-C5
Wheeler • 1,584	5-B6
Wheelock	16-A4
White Deer 1,210	4-B4
Whiteface 463	7-A7
Whiteflat	5-D5
Whitehouse 2,172	11-C6
Whitely	4-D4
White Oak	11-C6
Whitesboro 3,197	9-A8
White Settlement 13,508	24-D1
Whitewright 1,760	10-A4
Whitharral	4-D3
Whitney 1,631	9-C8
Whitsett	15-D7
Whitt	9-B7
Wichita Falls • 94,201	5-D8,28-E3
Wickett 689	7-C6
Wied	16-C3
Wildorado	4-B3
Wilkinson	11-B6
Willis 1,674	17-B6
Willow City	15-B6
Willow Park	9-B7
Wills Point 2,631	11-B5
Wilmer 2,367	10-C4,25-F7
Wilmeth	8-C4
Wilson 578	8-A2
Wimberly	15-B7
Winchell	9-D5
Winchester	16-B3
Windcrest	29-C7
Windom	10-A4
Windthorst 409	9-A6
Wingate	8-C4
Wink 1,182	7-C6
Winnie	17-B7
Winnsboro 3,458	11-B5
Winona 443	11-C6
Winter Haven	14-D4
Winters 3,061	8-C4
Wise	10-C4
Woden	11-D7
Wolfe City 1,594	10-B4
Wolfforth 1,701	7-A8
Womack	9-C8
Woodlake	17-A6
Woodland	11-A5
Woodlands, The	17-B5
Woodlawn	11-B7
Woodrow	7-A8
Woodsboro 1,974	19-A6
Woodson 291	9-B5
Woodville • 2,821	17-A7
Wortham 1,187	10-D4
Wrightsboro	15-C8
Wyne	10-B4
Yancey	15-D5
Yantis 210	11-B5
Yoakum 6,148	16-C3
Yorktown 2,498	15-D8
Zapata •	18-C3
Zavalla 762	17-A7
Zephyr	9-C6
Zorn	15-C7

IV-583-J-XA

City Maps

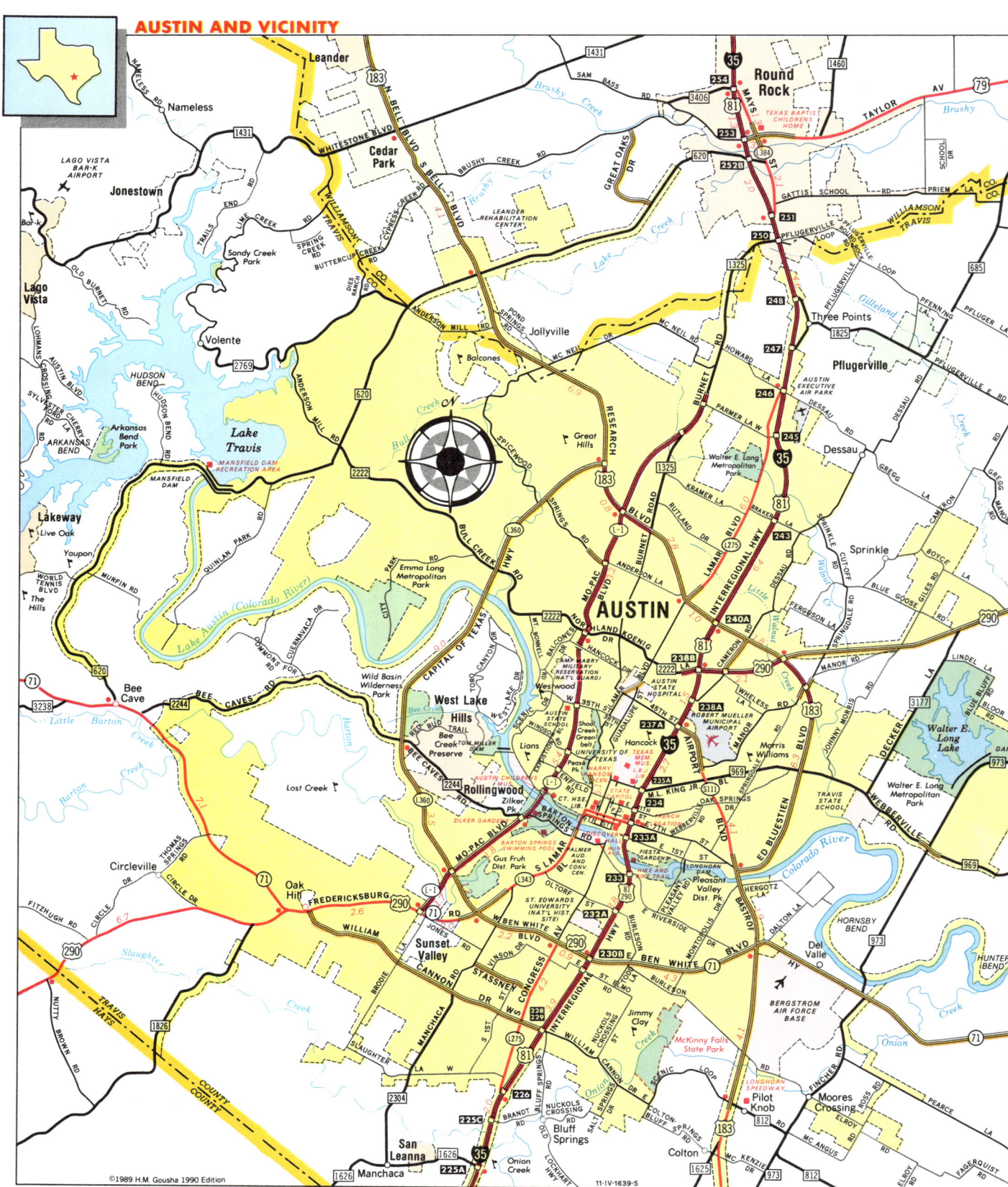

AUSTIN AND VICINITY

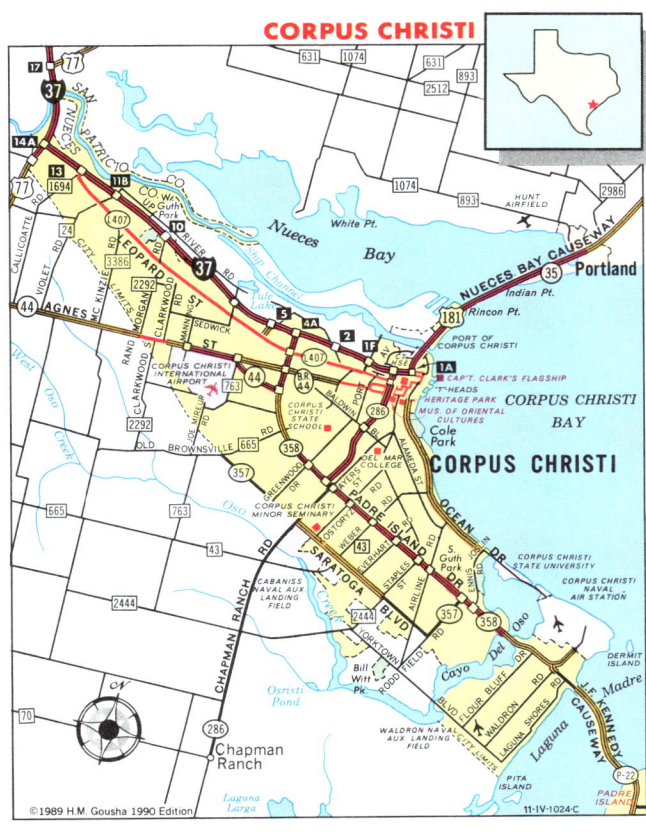

DALLAS AND VICINITY

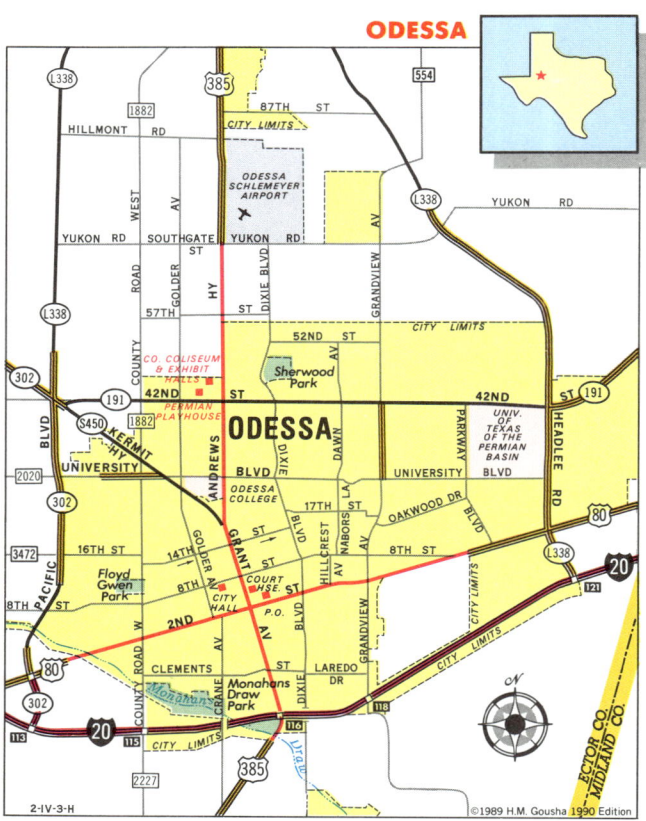
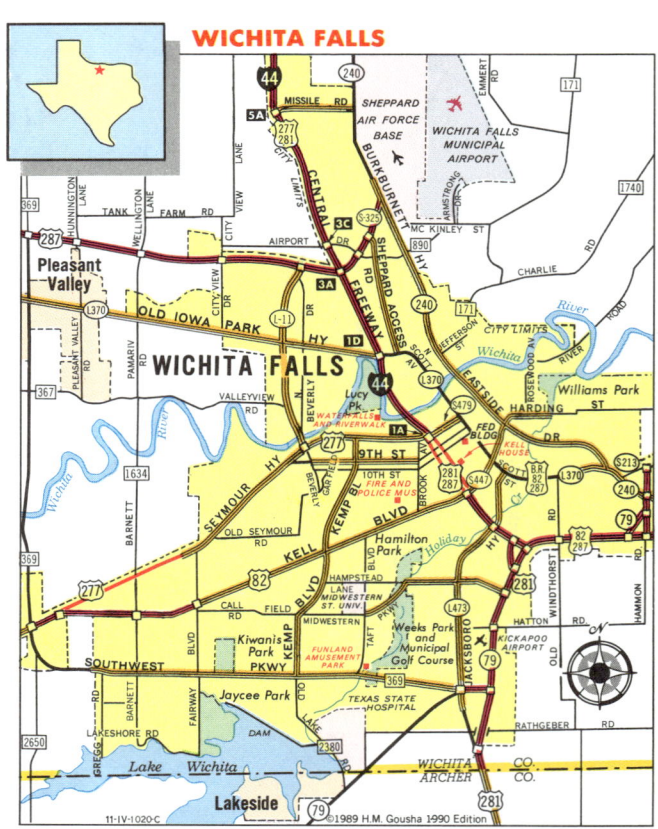

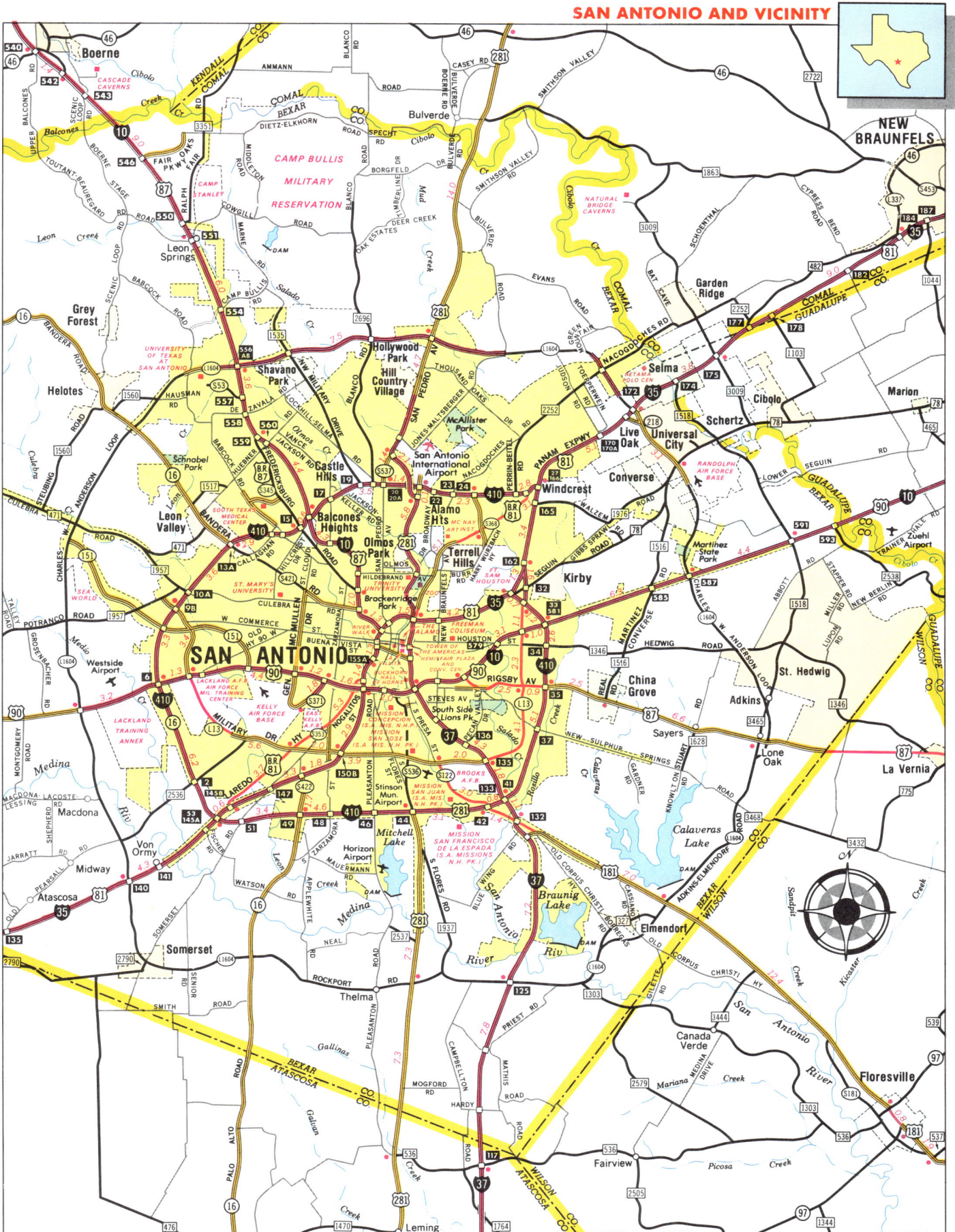

Discovering TEXAS

When the Republic of Texas joined the United States in 1845, after gaining its independence from Mexico at the Battle of Jacinto in 1836, it maintained the right to divide into five separate states. That right was never exercised. However, today there exist six imaginary boundaries which divide the state by region; these are most likely the borders that would have been used had Texas separated. Texans refer to these regions as: East Texas or the Piney Woods, Central Texas or Hill Country, South Texas or the Gulf Coast, North Central Texas or the Metroplex, the Panhandle and West Texas. Considering Texas' size–over 275,416 square miles–the state is perhaps most easily comprehended by territory. Although there are some obvious differences in terrain among the regions, they share a common history, culture, lifestyle and tradition. No region is any more significant or "Texan" than the other; together they all make up the great state of Texas.

EAST TEXAS/ PINEY WOODS

East Texas earned its nickname, the "Piney Woods," from the dense forests that sweep north from the Louisiana border. The region is especially beautiful in the spring when the Dogwood trees and wildflowers bloom. Four National Forests, over 11 million acres of "Piney Woods," and 50,000 miles of sumptuous greenery are located in East Texas. **The Big Thicket National Preserve** is an 84,500 acre enclave protecting rare and indigenous foliage and birds. On the northern edge of the Preserve is the **Alabama-Coushatta Reservation**, Texas' largest Indian reservation.

East Texas is steeped in history. When Spanish explorers arrived there in the 16th century, they discovered the remarkably civilized and prosperous Caddo Indians.

> Whenever possible, Points of Interest are located on the state and city maps that appear on pages 4–29, and they are referenced in the text by a page number and map coordinates enclosed in parenthesis (example: p. 4,D–3). If the Point of Interest is not spotted on the state map, the listing will include the map coordinates for the city in which it is located.

The explorers converted the Caddo word for friends into "Tejas," thus giving Texas its name and its motto—Friendship. Centuries later, Anglo pioneer Stephen F. Austin, "the Father of Texas," began colonizing East Texas despite the violence and unrest there during Texas' fight for independence. Today, the region is noted for its scenic beauty, brilliant fall foliage and friendly Southern towns.

Notable Sights in East Texas

BEAUMONT is the birthplace of the petroleum industry in the United States. In 1901, after years of prospecting and close to giving up, Patillo Higgins finally hit "black gold" at **Spindletop.** Oil spewed 150 feet in the air for several days, proving that vast quantities existed below the ground. Also of note is the **McFaddin-Ward House**, a colonial mansion featuring a fine collection of period furnishings and silver. (p. 17, B–7)

COLLEGE STATION is the home of Texas A&M University. Originally founded as a military school, ("A" stands for agriculture, "M" for military) it is one of the nation's 10 largest schools. (p. 16, A–4)

JEFFERSON is a remarkably well-preserved township with over 100 pre-Civil War homes. **The Excelsior House**, a 19th century boarding house visited by Ulysses S. Grant and Oscar Wilde, among others, still operates. (p. 11, B–7)

NACOGDOCHES was the site of an Indian settlement for centuries before it was visited by the Spanish explorer La Salle in 1687. Of particular interest is **The Old Stone Fort**, built in 1779 as a trading post, later the headquarters for two early, unsuccessful attempts to establish the Republic of Texas. Nacogdoches is also the home of Texas' first newspaper, printed in 1812. (p. 11, D–6)

TYLER is a hospitable southern town where over one-third of the country's commercial roses are grown. **The Municipal Rose Garden** is the nation's largest showcase of roses, boasting 40,000 plants in 500 varieties from May through October. (p. 11, C–5)

CENTRAL TEXAS/ THE HILL COUNTRY

Central Texas is known as "The Heart of Texas" but it gets its popular moniker, "The Hill Country," from its topography. The Hill Country is a land of gently rolling limestone hills. Numerous creeks and springs still sculpt the land and nourish an abundance of trees and native wildflowers. Water, in the form of spring-fed rivers and streams, is the region's most valuable natural resource. The bluebonnets (the State Flower) and Mexican Paintbrushes that blanket the Hill Country in the spring make the region one of the most breath-taking and serene in all of Texas.

Like much of Texas, the Hill Country's charm lies in its quaint small towns, friendly inhabitants and long, lazy backroads. Lakes such as Buchanan and Travis provide recreation and ideal picnicking opportunities. Hill Country towns participate in the Bluebonnet Trail in the spring when flowers festoon the hills, providing an impressive backdrop for a lavish festival featuring music, food, crafts and fun!

The major cities of **San Antonio** and **Austin** are an integral part of Central Texas and will be discussed in detail later.

Notable Sights in Central Texas

BANDERA is known for its many guest and dude ranches. Some are rustic and some luxurious but all provide swimming, horseback riding and family fun. The Chamber of Commerce, (512) 796-3045, can provide a complete list of ranches open to visitors. (p. 15, C–6)

BURNET is one of the ancient geological areas of the world, captivating both renowned geologists and amateur rock collectors. It's premiere attraction is the **Vanishing Texas River Cruise**, a tour boat journey of the Hill Country's wildlife and scenery along 23,000 acre Lake Buchanan. Burnet is also noted for its excellent fishing and golf. (p. 15, A–7)

KERRVILLE is dotted with summer camps and guest ranches. **The Cowboy Artists of America Museum** features work by the finest living Western artists, many of whom live on the property. (p. 15, B–5)

FREDRICKSBURG is rich with German tradition, culture and cuisine. The town is known for its **Sunday Houses**, built for ranchers who came into town for church on Sundays. **The Admiral Nimitz Museum** houses exhibits from the life of Chester Nimitz, a native son who was Commander-in-Chief of the Pacific during World War II. (p. 15, B–6)

WACO, a major industrialized city, is an up-and-coming destination for tourists. **The Texas Ranger Hall of Fame** chronicles the history and heritage of the Rangers with an impressive collection of guns, Western art and artifacts from the Old West. (p. 10, D–3)

SOUTH TEXAS/ THE GULF COAST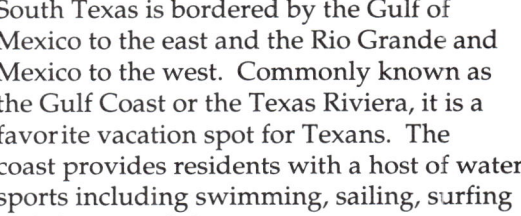

South Texas is bordered by the Gulf of Mexico to the east and the Rio Grande and Mexico to the west. Commonly known as the Gulf Coast or the Texas Riviera, it is a favorite vacation spot for Texans. The coast provides residents with a host of water sports including swimming, sailing, surfing and deep-sea fishing.

The major cities of **Houston** and **Galveston** are considered part of South Texas and will be examined in detail later. The seaside resort town of **Corpus Christi** is also detailed in a later section.

TEXAS TIME★LINE

1519
A strip of land along the Gulf from Florida to Mexico is declared a Spanish colony. The Texas coastline was first mapped by Alonso Alvarez de Pineda, who named Corpus Christi Bay.

1685
Explorer Sieur de la Salle claimed Matagorda Bay and the surrounding area for France.

1721
Spanish explorer Marques de Aguayo established the capital of the Spanish colony of Texas at Los Adaes in East Texas near the Louisiana border.

1821
Moses Austin was granted permission from the Spanish to establish an Anglo settlement in East Texas, a colony now known as "the old three hundred." He died before he could get the project underway but his son, Stephen F. Austin carried out the plan and is

(continued)

Notable Sights in South Texas

BROWNSVILLE is noted for its semi-tropical climate and proximity to Mexico and South Padre Island. At **The Gladys Porter Zoo**, 1,500 rare and exotic animals are displayed in natural settings. (p. 19, D–6)

PADRE ISLAND is the nation's largest barrier island stretching along the Texas coast from Corpus Christi to the Rio Grande. Most of Padre's 113-mile length is designated as National Seashore and boasts spectacular beaches and dunes. The southern tip, **South Padre Island**, is a busy seaside resort town. South Padre Island is also a favorite destination for Texas college students during Spring Break. (p. 19, C–6)

PORT ARANSAS is one of the most popular tourist stops along the Texas Riviera. Settled as a fishing village in the mid 19th century, the town still promotes itself as a place "where they bite every day." Free fishing is available, and the large variety of native species include redfish and sand trout. There are also opportunities for deep sea fishing and a full calendar of fishing tournaments. (p. 19, A–7)

ROCKPORT is an important commercial fishing area on a peninsula sheltered from the Gulf by San Jose Island. The **Aransas National Wildlife Refuge**, located 12-miles across the bay, is a winter retreat for 300 species of exotic birds including the near-extinct whooping crane. This is an ideal spot for nature lovers and bird-watchers. (p.19, A–7)

NORTH CENTRAL TEXAS/ THE METROPLEX

North Central Texas is known as The Metroplex; here, the sprawling cities of Dallas and Fort Worth are joined by a maze of highways. (Both **Dallas** and **Fort Worth** are treated in detail later.) The Metroplex, as its name indicates, is largely composed of slate, granite and steel structures. The area is largely industrialized and lacks any navigable waterways or natural resources such as oil or timber. However, nearby lakes and reservoirs provide an escape for city dwellers as well as crucial water supply to the urban hubs. There are also a number of state parks that offer local recreation.

Notable Sights in North Central Texas

ARLINGTON came into existence around 1876 when the railroad arrived. Until the mid 1940s it was an agricultural center but since then has grown in business, industry and recreation. Arlington is the home of the American League **Texas Rangers** Baseball team. **Six Flags Over Texas** is a lavish 200 acre amusement park featuring rides, musical reviews, shows and restaurants. (p. 24, D–4)

GRAND PRAIRIE is widely noted for its **Traders Village**, a huge weekend flea market with exhibitors selling antiques, arts and crafts, plants, and all types of handmade goods. The **International Wildlife Park** is a drive-through preserve featuring elephants, rhinos, giraffes and other exotic animals imported from Africa for breeding and preservation. (p. 25, D–5)

IRVING is located in the center of many of the attractions of the Metroplex and is convenient to Dallas/Fort Worth Airport. A thriving industrial and residential community, it is home to the legendary **Dallas Cowboys**. The **Las Colinas Complex** is a modern 12,000 acre multi-use facility including an equestrian center, movie studio, hotels, shops and restaurants. Las Colinas is famous for artist Robert Glen's monumental bronze sculpture of nine mustangs galloping through water. (p. 25, C–5)

THE PANHANDLE

Bordered by New Mexico to the west and Oklahoma to the north and east, the Panhandle is part of America's Great Plains. The region is flat, arid and relatively undeveloped. The economy is centered in the major cities of **Amarillo** (detailed in a later section) and Lubbock where ranching, cotton and sunflower seed harvesting are the major industries. In mid-summer, the bluebonnets that blanket the Hill Country reach the Panhandle for a short time.

Countless towns such as Pamp and Panhandle sprang up in the late 1800s as working camps for the laborers who laid the Santa Fe Railroad track. Later, settlers found cheap grazing for their cattle, and the railheads and stockyards became a lucrative business despite the frequently sweltering temperatures and rugged terrain of the Panhandle.

Today the Panhandle retains its Old West spirit. It is populated by friendly, hardworking people who make custom guns, saddles, hats and boots. Country music is a way of life here and the Panhandle is proud of native sons like Waylon Jennings, Mac Davis and Lubbock's Buddy Holly.

Notable Sights in Panhandle

LUBBOCK, one of the larger cities in the South Plains, is a center for manufacturing, agribusiness and the petroleum industry. More

---

generally credited as being "The Father of Texas." Stephen F. Austin died in December of 1836, just after Texas won its independence from Mexico.

1836
For thirteen days in March the Battle at the Alamo was fought. Davy Crockett, Jim Bowie, and William Travis vowed to fight "'till victory or death." They and all their men perished at the hands of the Mexicans.

1836
On April 21, Texas independence was secured at the Battle of San Jacinto. General Sam Houston led the battle which lasted only 18 minutes, and in which 950 Texans captured 700 Mexicans. Houston went on to be elected president of the Republic of Texas (twice), U.S. Senator and Governor. He died in 1863 and his gravestone reads, "The world shall take care of Sam Houston's fame."

1845
Texas became the 28th state on the condition that it could divide itself into five separate states if it chose to do so. It also retained ownership of all federal lands and to this day any Texan land owned by the U.S. government was bought or given to them.

1850
For $10 million, the U.S. government bought 98,300 square miles of territory from the new state which included parts of New Mexico, Colorado, Oklahoma, Kansas and Wyoming.

1861
Texas seceded from the Union making the Confederate flag the sixth to fly over Texas. Sam Houston was removed as governor when he refused to pledge alliegence to the Confederacy.

recently, Lubbock has begun producing wine. Lubbock is also a cultural center, boasting a symphony, ballet and the **Lubbock Fine Arts Center** which features changing exhibits on contemporary art. **Mackenzie State Park** attracts more visitors than any other Texas state park and features a rare Prairie Dog colony. (p. 8, A–1)

ABILENE was established as a cattle shipping point in 1881 and later became a large cattle producing area. The discovery of oil buttressed the growing local economy; today, manufacturing and agriculture are other economic mainstays. **Dyess Air Force Base** displays classic and ultra-modern aircraft including the B17 "Flying Fortress". **The Abilene Fine Arts Museum** offers revolving exhibits from the Old Masters to the modern and abstract arts. Abilene has two lakes that offer picnic facilities, fishing and swimming. (p. 8, B–4)

MINERAL WELLS was made famous in the late 1800s by the claim that local resident J. A. Lynch's well had medicinal qualities that could cure a variety of ailments. Health-seekers flocked to the area. Today, tourists are drawn to the balmy climate and picturesque surroundings. **Lake Mineral Wells State Park** is made up of over 2,800 acres including a large lake with opportunities for fishing, boating and camping. (p. 9, B–7)

WICHITA FALLS has a wild, reckless history. Most of it was won by Louisiana financier John C. Scott in a 1873 poker game in New Orleans. The deeds to the land lay untouched for 17 years until Scott's heirs learned the railroad would be coming through. In 1882 it finally arrived and the town prospered. Today, the economy is largely oil-related with some farming and ranching. **Kell House** contains the elegant home furnishings of local 19th century businessman Frank Kell. (p. 10, A–1)

WEST TEXAS

While much of Texas is not what you'd expect — the rolling hills and wildflowers of the Hill Country, the dense lush forests of the Piney Woods — West Texas is largely what you *would* expect: huge ranches, incomparable sunsets and vast, hot, dry desert. However, there are surprises. Though much of West Texas is flat and arid, **Davis Mountains State Park** is a serene mountain setting. Wide-open spaces, mile-high mountains and natural beauty abound in the two national parks that are located here. At **Big Bend National Park** you can float or raft down the Rio Grande or hike through over 240 miles of trails. The **Guadalupe Mountains National Park** boasts a series of high peaks, deep canyons and natural pools that are a far cry from the prevailing character of West Texas. (See page 43 for more information.)

The history of West Texas is rich with cowboys and Indians, duels and gunfights. The cities of West Texas are steeped in Mexican, Spanish and Indian traditions, and retain a rugged, outdoor appeal.

Notable Sights in West Texas

FORT DAVIS NATIONAL HISTORIC SITE is dramatically situated amid high mountains and flowing streams. Fort Davis was a southwestern frontier post established to protect travelers using the San Antonio–El Paso Road. It played a major role in opening up the west to settlers. (p. 13, B–5)

MIDLAND was named for its location between Fort Worth and El Paso. It was originally agricultural, but since the discovery of oil in the Permian Basin, has become a center for the West Texas oil industry. **The Permian Basin Petroleum Museum** is the largest museum of its kind devoted to the history of the oil industry; it exhibits early photos, well-drilling techniques and related memorabilia. (p. 7, C–8)

PECOS, founded in 1881 as a stop on the Texas and Pacific Railroad, was a rowdy cowboy town, a favorite of such outlaws as Billy the Kid. Pecos claims to be "Home of the World's First Rodeo" and it continues to celebrate its century-old annual rodeo. The **West-of-the-Pecos Museum** occupies an old saloon and the historic **Orient Hotel** depicts the region's colorful frontier history. Pecos is also known for its Pecos Cantaloupes which are harvested from late July through September and are considered among the world's best. (p. 7, D–6)

TERLINGUA is one of Texas' best known ghost towns. A true boom town, its population grew to 2,000 in the 1880s with prospectors extracting cinnabar and mercury from the ground. When the minerals were depleted, the inhabitants moved on. One of Texas' great traditions, **The World's Championship Chili Cook-Off** started here in 1967 and draws over 5,000 chili chefs and aficionados from all over the world during the first weekend in November. (Most attendee's bring tents or campers since there are no accommodations in Terlingua and very few in the surrounding areas.) (p. 13, D–5)

1908
On August 27, Lyndon Baines Johnson was born near the Pedernales River in Hill Country. He went on to serve in the Texas legislature, the U.S. House of Representatives, the U.S. Senate, and was the first president to claim Texas as his home. In 1937, he won his first of six congressional terms and in 1948 he won his first senate seat by only 87 votes. In November of 1963 he became our 36th president, and in 1969 he left office, ending a career in public life that spanned over 40 years.

1923
University of Texas-owned Santa Rita No. 1 strikes oil at 3,050 feet and frees the university from legislative restraints and budgetary limitations.

1924
Texas elects a woman governor, Miriam "Ma" Ferguson; it is the first state to do so.

1975
December 28 was the date of the most famous play in Dallas Cowboy history: Roger Staubach's Hail Mary pass to Drew Pearson to beat the Minnesota Vikings.

1978
Best Little Whorehouse in Texas opens off-Broadway to enthusiastic reviews.

1981
Henry Cisneros becomes mayor of San Antonio; he is the first Mexican-American to be elected mayor of one of the nation's ten largest cities.

CITY LIFE

Texas is larger than life. It is oil fields and ranches, longhorns and urban cowboys, *Lonesome Dove* and *Dallas*. But it is also small towns and skyscrapers, a haven for the arts, with vast stretches of flat desert, formidable mountains, lush forests and unspoiled coastline. The state's tourism department bills Texas, quite accurately, "Like A Whole Other Country." If you're looking for deserts and frontier towns, they've got 'em, sophisticated opera and "yuppified" neighborhoods, no problem. Texas does not disappoint. It's everything you've imagined and everything you haven't.

This section highlights eight major cities in Texas, focusing on the history, character and major attractions of each city. If you are planning a trip to one of these cities, contact the Texas Tourism Department in Austin. They are extremely helpful and can send up-to-date tourist information to help you plan every aspect of your trip (Texas Department of Commerce, 816 Congress St., P.O. Box 12728, Austin, TX 78711. (512) 320-9414).

GOING TO TOWN IN TEXAS

AUSTIN

"Gentlemen, this should be the seat of the future Empire!", stated Mirabeau Bonaparte Lamar in 1838 when he chose Austin as Texas' capital. Then the vice president of the Republic of Texas, Lamar had good taste. He appreciated the central location, pleasant climate and the natural beauty of the Colorado River Valley, the center of the Hill Country, liberally peppered with creeks, lakes and lush, rolling hills.

Austin was named after Stephen F. Austin, originally a Virginian who settled in East Texas along with 300 families. Austin is generally regarded as "the Father of Texas." Though the capital was temporarily moved to Houston during Sam Houston's administration, the government was officially and permanently moved back to Austin in 1844, shortly before Texas became part of the United States. Austin's link with the rest of the state was strengthened in the early 1870s, with the installation of telegraph lines and the arrival of the railroad. Austin's dominance grew with the increasing role of the state government and the intellectual leverage of the University of Texas (UT).

Today Austinites revel in the city's beauty, history and cultural offerings. Running is a popular sport and the Hike and Bike Trail, developed by Lady Bird Johnson, winds around Town Lake and provides 8.5 miles of well-groomed trails in the center of town. Music is almost a religion here and live music of all kinds is performed locally every night. (For a roundup of live music venues around the state, see p. 54). The excitement of the state government is omnipresent even when the legislature is not in session. UT provides the liberal influence and intellectual stimulation that make the city one of the state's most exhilarating. (*See Austin city map, p. 22*)

DON'T MISS

Austin Convention and Visitor's Bureau, (512) 478-0098

State Capitol Complex - The pink marble Capitol building is Austin's most familiar architectural landmark. Free guided tours of the beautiful buildings and immaculately landscaped grounds provide an excellent starting point for discovering the history of Texas. Note that the Texas flag flies at the same height as the U. S. flag, a symbolic gesture of which Texans are very proud. Open 24 hours, tours daily 8:15 - 4:30, Capitol Square. Free. (*p. 22, E–3*)

University of Texas - In 1858 state lawmakers bestowed UT with state owned farmland but later took back the valuable, mineral-rich land and replaced it with 2 million acres in West Texas that were thought to be almost worthless. In 1923, Santa Rita No. 1, a drilling rig on UT land, struck oil and today UT's oil endowment is over 3 billion dollars. The financial security that the oil has provided has freed UT from legislative budgets and contributed to the rich culture and reputation of the university. Many of Austin's premiere attractions are located on the UT grounds. Start with the Visitors Center at 709 E. Martin Luther King Blvd. which has a staff that will help you plan your tour. Daily, 8 - 4:30. (512) 471-1420. (*p. 22, D–3*)

Lyndon B. Johnson Library and Museum - Archives and mementos of LBJ's long political career including gifts from heads of state and a replica of LBJ's Oval Office. Exhibits detail Johnson's years in Congress, "The Great Society" and the Vietnam War. Of special interest is a letter written to LBJ from Jacqueline Kennedy the day after her husband's funeral. 9-5 daily. UT Campus, 2313 Red River Street. Free. (512) 482-5136. (*p. 22, E–3*)

Harry Ransom Center - Located on the University of Texas (UT) campus, it houses the renowned Michener Collection of over 300 selections of American Art. UT Campus, 21st and Guadalupe. M-Sa 9-5, Su 1-5. Admission. (512) 471-8944. (*p. 22, E–3*)

Texas Memorial Museum - This museum houses historical and geological artifacts and exhibits that are unique to Texas. M-F 9-5, Sa 10-5, Su 1-5. UT Campus, 2400 Trinity Street. Free. (512) 471-1604. (*p. 22, E–3*)

French Legation - Built in 1840 by the French charge d'affaires to the Republic of Texas, it is an outstanding example of Creole architecture and contains a valuable collection of period furnishings. Tu - Su 1-5. 802 San Marcos St. Admission. (512) 472-8180. (*p. 22, E–3*)

Sixth Street (Old Pecan Street) - Before the capitol was built, this was Austin's main street. Its classic Victorian and stone buildings now house a festival of diverse restaurants, shops, galleries and clubs and is reminiscent of Georgetown in Washington, D. C. 7 blocks between I-35 and Congress Avenue. (*p. 22, E–3*)

Barton Springs Pool - This natural pool, fed by the cool, refreshing springs of the Hill Country, has been open to the public since 1920. Located in one of the city's most widely used recreation areas, Zilker Park, the pool ranges from ankle deep to 15 feet. Its unusually frigid waters attract the Polar Bear Club for daily swims all year long. It is open 24 hours year-round. In the winter, swimmers swim at their own risk. 2100 Barton Springs Road, Free. (512) 476-9044. (*p. 22, E–3*)

Zilker Gardens - Also located in Zilker Park, the gardens offer a huge variety of native flowering plants as well as an impressive rose garden. Perhaps most beautiful of all is the Oriental Garden, a peaceful oasis of footpaths, oriental flowers, water lilies and wooden bridges. Daily, 2220 Barton Springs Road. (512) 477-8672. Free. (*p. 22, E–3*)

SAN ANTONIO

Remember the Alamo—but don't forget to visit the Riverwalk and the other unique features of Texas' most European-looking city. Discovered by a troop of soldiers and missionaries on Saint Anthony of Padua's feast day in 1691, it is one of Texas' most historic cities. The Indians who lived there were not joined by white settlers until 1718 when the San Antonio de Valero Mission—later known as the Alamo—was erected.

Through the rest of the 1700s and the early part of the 1800s, colonization and the conversion of the Indians took place with the onslaught of Anglo migration. When Texas began to break from Mexico to later become the Republic of Texas in 1837, the city endured constant attacks from Mexico and the Indians. Visitors to San Antonio are reminded of Davy Crockett and a small band of men who fought to their deaths in 1836 against several thousand Mexican soldiers in the Republic's most infamous battle, The Alamo.

Today visitors are delighted by the city's old world charm and Mexican ambiance. The Riverwalk, a two mile stretch of the narrow San Antonio River, is dotted with galleries, shops and restaurants. The sidewalk cafes and hotel balconies overlooking the river lend the city some of Venice's character. When you're in San Antonio you can't help but appreciate the meshing of Mexican, Spanish and American culture in the food, the history, the music and the people. (*See San Antonio city map, p. 29*)

DON'T MISS

San Antonio Convention and Visitors Bureau, (512) 270-8700

The Alamo - The old mission turned fort is a poignant monument to the 188 men who died fighting for Texas independence against thousands of Mexican soldiers in a 13 day battle. The phrase "Remember the Alamo!" is credited to General Sam Houston who later defeated the Mexicans at San Jacinto to finally win Texas' freedom. Alamo at Houston Streets, M-Sa 9-5:30, Su 10-5:30. Free. (512) 225-1693. (*p. 29, D–6*)

Riverwalk (Paseo Del Rio) - The Riverwalk is to San Antonio what the U. S. Capitol or the Washington Monument is to Washington, D.C.; it's what people come to San Antonio to see and keep coming back for. Located downtown along the San Antonio River, it is open all the time. Free. (*p. 29, D–6*)

San Antonio Missions National Historical Park - Four of San Antonio's five 18th century Spanish missions, located at different spots along the San Antonio River, make up the park. Open seven days, 9-6 summer, 8-5 winter. Free. (512) 229-5701. (*p. 29, D–6*)

La Villita - The city began here in the mid 1700s. In the 1830s, the tiny adobe cottages housed the missionaries and soliders that founded the city. Today, the dwellings make up a charming village of artisans, restaurants and shops. Three blocks south of The Alamo on Alamo Street. Open 24 hours. Free. (*p. 29, D–6*)

San Antonio Zoo - One of the finest zoos in the country, it is noted for its natural settings, creative exhibits, exotic animals and one of the world's largest bird collections. Brackenridge Park on N. St. Mary's Street, seven days, 9:30-6:30. Admission. (512) 734-7183. (*p. 29, C–6*)

Sea World of Texas - The world's largest marine life exhibit includes "Shamu" the killer whale, dolphin and sea lion shows, Antarctic penguins and special displays and attractions that take over eight hours to see! Ellison Dr. and Westover Hills Blvd, open seven days, various hours. Admission. (512) 523-3000 or toll free (800)422-7989. (p. 29, C–5)

Tower of the Americas - Built for the 1968 World's Fair, the 750 feet-high tower provides the best panoramic view of San Antonio and its environs. On a clear day, you can see the rolling terrain of the Hill Country. HemisFair Plaza near E.Market, open seven days, 10am-11pm. Admission (512) 299-8615. (p. 29, D–6)

McNay Art Museum - The small but diverse collection including Impressionist, Medieval and Southwestern art and sculpture, is in the Spanish style estate of founder, Marian Koogler McNay. 600 N. New Braunfels at Austin Highway, Tu-Sa 9-5, Sun 2-5. Free. (512) 824-5368. (p. 29, C–6)

Buckhorn Hall of Horns - An unusual but popular tourist spot, the Hall of Horns is a staggering display of antlers and mounted animals including a record-breaking longhorn. 600 Lone Star Boulevard at Mission Road, open seven days, 9:30-5. Admission. (512) 270-9469. (p. 29, D–6)

DALLAS

"Big D" was founded in 1840 when Arkansas native John Neely Brown settled here and opened a humble trading post on the banks of the Trinity River. Like many western and southwestern cities, Dallas found its way onto maps with the arrival of the Texas Central Railroad in 1872 and the Texas and Pacific Line in 1873. The railroads brought commerce, business and entrepreurship.

Dallas' economy has been diversified from the start and although oil money is a factor, it is not the foundation. Since World War II, the city's economy has relied on the insurance business (Dallas is the nation's third largest insurance center), film production, fashion and conventioneers. It also leads the southwest in transportation, electronics, and computer technology; the computer chip was invented here in 1958.

Among other cultural offerings, the city boasts an impressive art museum, opera company, symphony orchestra and world-class hotels and restaurants. Dallas just keeps on growing, relatively undaunted by the fall in oil prices in the early 1980s. You can't go to far without seeing a construction site paving "Big D's" way into the future—the city expects its population of 976,598 to double by the year 2000! (*See Dallas city map, p. 25*)

DON'T MISS
Dallas Convention and Visitors Bureau, (214) 746-6679

Fair Park - Home of the country's oldest annual state fair, the Park's 277 acres are registered as a National Historic Landmark. Much of the Park was built in 1936 for the state's Centennial celebration. For two weeks every October since 1886, the Dallas State Fair is held here. The park contains several wonderful museums including the Dallas Museum of Natural History, The Dallas Aquarium and the Dallas Civic Garden Center. Entrance on Parry Avenue. Open daily. (*p. 25, D–7*)

Dallas Museum of Art - The museum has a fine collection of paintings and sculpture but is particularly noted for its unusual exhibits of pre-Columbian and African art. The Reeves Collection is a $35-million dollar collection of furnishings and porcelains with a special room devoted to Winston Churchill's artwork and memorabilia. 1717 N. Harwood, Tu-Sa 10-5, Th 10-9, Su 12-5. Admission fee charged for some exhibits. (214) 922-1200. (*p. 25, C–7*)

West End Historic District and West End Marketplace - This renovated warehouse and business district is teeming with boutiques, clubs, shops, craftsmen and restaurants. Opportunities for shoppers, tourists and nightowls abound. Downtown Market Street from Elm to Munyor. (*p. 25, D–7*)

Biblical Arts Center - One of the most unusual attractions anywhere. Non-denominational, it features religious paintings, sculpture and artifacts from around the world including a replica of Christ's tomb. The highlight is the world's largest oil painting (120' x 20') depicting the Miracle at Pentecost accompanied by a dramatic, 30-minute sound and light show. 7500 Park Lane at Boedeker Street, Tu-Sa 10-5, Su 1-5. Free admission to the gallery, admission fee charged for the presentation of "The Miracle at Pentecost." (214) 691-4661. (*p. 25, C–7*)

JFK Memorials - Few visitors to Dallas pass through without visiting the spot where President John F. Kennedy was assassinated on November 22, 1963. The infamous Schoolbook Depository on the corner of Houston and Elm is where Lee Harvey Oswald allegedly fired the fatal shots. A permanent exhibit on JFK's life and career is scheduled to open there this year. There is also a historical marker honoring the late President on Houston Street. Nearby is the grassy knoll and Triple Underpass, indelible memories of that sad day. (*p. 25, D–7*)

Thanks-Giving Square - This nondenominational "square" is really a triangle commissioned by the city in the 1970s and designed by architect Philip Johnson. It provides a tranquil escape among waterfalls and landscaped grounds for the city's busy residents. Its descending walkways gives visitors a chance to reflect and relax. Bordered by Bryan, Ervay and Pacific. (*p. 25, D–7*)

Southfork Ranch - Guided tours are available of the mansion and ranch made famous by the television program *Dallas*. A 183 foot oil rig and ranch animals are also located on the grounds. Located several miles northeast of downtown of FM 2551. Daily 9-dusk. Admission. (214) 442-6536. (*p. 10, B–4*)

FORT WORTH

Fort Worth is allied with its Metroplex neighbor, Dallas, only geographically. They share the same airport (Dallas/Fort Worth Airport is larger than the island of Manhattan) and highways but both cities are quick to point out that they are *not* "sister cities." While Dallas considers itself glamorous and urbane, Fort Worth has always been "Cowtown," and proud of it.

Fort Worth, though never a fort, was originally settled in 1849 by Major Ripley Arnold and the 42 men of Company F to protect Dallas and other eastern settlements from Indian attack. Arnold named the outpost in honor of General William J. Worth, a hero of the Mexican War. In the early years, soldiers watched for enemy assault from the bluffs overlooking the Trinity River while cowboys drove their herds along the Chisholm Trail below. This was the last stop on the trail before the cowboys made it into Oklahoma and Indian Territory, so they whooped-it-up here before pushing their charges along the next lonely, 300-mile stretch.

In the 1870s, downtown Fort Worth evolved into "Hell's Half-Acre," a mini-boomtown of swinging-door saloons , brothels, gambling and shoot-outs for adventure-seeking cowboys such as Wyatt Earp and Butch Cassidy. In 1876 the railroad arrived and secured Fort Worth as a main cattle shipping point for ranchers. Soon, Swift and Armour, two Chicago meat-packing companies set up shop here. Stockyards and rodeos came next and Fort Worth earned its enduring nickname, Cowtown. In the early part of the 20th century, oil was discovered in nearby counties and Fort Worth lost it's shoot-'em-up frontier town character.

Today Fort Worth promotes itself as "The Way You Want Texas to Be" and still has the authentic feeling of the Old West. Oil has overtaken cattle as the most important industry, but there are still rodeos, saloons and live country music. Cowtown is not as unsophisticated as its neighbor would have you think. Its impressive cultural offerings include museums, galleries, a symphony and ballet. (*See Fort Worth city map, p. 24*)

DON'T MISS
Fort Worth Convention and Visitor's Bureau, (817) 336-8791

Fort Worth Stockyards - Thousands of cowboys have driven their millions of livestock up Main Street over the last century and the Fort Worth Stockyards are still operational. Today, visitors to the stockyard can recapture the Old West in one of the state's most authentically "Texan" attractions. Main Street and Exchange Avenue, M-Sa 10-5:30, Su 12-6. Free. (817) 624-4741. (*p. 24, D–2*)

Amon C. Carter Museum of Western Art - Amon C. Carter was a Fort Worth newspaper publisher and philanthropist who donated his collection and funding for a museum upon his death in 1955. Visitors can enjoy the paintings, sculpture and photography of the finest southwestern artists including Frederic Remington, Charles M. Russel, Ansel Adams and Georgia O'Keefe. 3501 Camp Bowie Boulevard, Tu-Sa 10-5, Su 1-5:30. Free. (817) 738-1933 (*p. 24, D–2*)

Eddleman - McFarland House Listed in the National Register of Historic Places, this elegant Victorian mansion is particularly noted for its elaborate woodwork. 1110 N. Penn. Admission. Tours by appointment only. (817) 332-5875. (*p. 24, D–2*)

Sundance Square - Fort Worth's downtown renovation project is named after the legendary Sundance Kid who, with Butch Cassidy of course, once hid out in Cowtown. The restored turn-of-the-century buildings in this charming historical district now contain a variety of shops, restaurants and galleries as well as lively nightspots. Bounded by W. 2nd, Houston, W. 4th and Commerce. For information call (817) 390-8711. (*p. 24, D–2*)

Fort Worth Botanical Gardens - 115 landscaped acres showcasing 150,000 plants of 2,500 species are on display in natural and formal settings. The highlight is the seven-and-a-half acre Japanese Garden known for its beauty and tranquility. 3220 Botanic Garden Drive (off University Drive). Open daily 8-11pm. Free. Admission fee charged for Japanese Garden only. (817) 870-7686. (*p. 24, D–2*)

Casa Manaña - A variety of Broadway shows are performed here on summer evenings in a 1,816 seat geodesic dome—one of the country's best theaters-in-the-round. 3101 W. Lancaster at University. Admission fees and show times vary. (817) 332-6221. (*p. 24, D–2*)

Cattleman's Museum - History of the longhorns and cowboys that were early Fort Worth are creatively displayed here. 1301 W. 7th M-F 8-5. Free. (817) 332-7064. (*p. 24, D–2*)

HOUSTON

New York land speculators Augustus and John Allen attracted settlers to this city by billing it as "The Next New Orleans" and an up-and-coming commercial port. The town was named after General Sam Houston in honor of his winning Texas independence at the Battle of San Jacinto. The city had an uneasy beginning but eventually lived up to its billing with the arrival of the railroad and the discovery of oil in southeast Texas in the early 1900s. After that, Houston grew. Lax zoning and planning laws throughout the 20th century have made it the largest city in the nation's largest state, spanning over 500 square miles.

Houston's livelihood was oil and when international oil prices dropped in 1983, the city and its environs entered a serious recession that still continues, although not as severely today. Though Houston is over 50 miles from the Gulf, it is the nation's fourth largest port. NASA's flight control and astronaut training facility is located here.

Many visitors remark that Houston "doesn't look like Texas." It is littered with skyscrapers, many of which are connected by underground tunnels because of the excessive heat and humidity most of the year. The city itself is a maze of highways not unlike Los Angeles, which requires Houstonians to own a car. The city is not all steel and cement though. If offers a wide range of visual and performing arts, excellent museums, theater and ballet. Houston really is "the big city" in Texas. (*See Houston city map, p. 26*)

DON'T MISS
Greater Houston Convention and Visitors Bureau, (713) 523-5050

Bayou Bend - The museum is operated under the auspices of the Museum of Fine Arts and is the former residence of the late Miss Ima Hogg who died in 1975 and was the only daughter of Governor James Hogg. The 28 room mansion is filled with American decorative arts from the colonial through the Victorian periods including paintings, furniture, silver and ceramics. The formal gardens and grounds are just as impressive with marble statues, fountains, waterfalls and a bird sanctuary. 1 Westcott St, Guided 90-minute tours by reservation only; children under 14 not permitted. Admission. (713) 529-8773. (*p. 26, C–2*)

San Jacinto Battleground State Park - This is the site of the famous Battle of San Jacinto where Sam Houston and his troops won Texas' independence from Mexico in a historic 18-minute battle. 21 miles from downtown Houston on Highway 225. Museum open daily, 9-6, Park 8-7. Free. (713) 479-2421. (*p. 27, A–5*)

Port of Houston - At the turn-of-the-century Houston widened its 50-mile ship channel and is now one of the world's busiest ports, the fourth largest in the U. S. Over 5,000 ships call here each year making Houston a hub for international commerce. Call (713) 225-4044 to arrange a tour. (*p. 27, B–7*)

LBJ Space Center - This is "Mission Control" and the headquarters of America's manned space program and the Space Shuttle project. Exhibits include spacecraft that travelled to the moon, lunar rocks, photos from Mars, examples of space technology and NASA satellites. 21 miles southeast of downtown on NASA Road 1 off of I-45. (713) 483-4321. Free. (*p. 27, C–5*)

Astrodomain - This huge entertainment complex includes Astrodome, Astrohall and Astroarena. Astrodome is the world's first indoor stadium and is the home of major league sports in Houston: the NFL's Houston Oilers and baseball's National League Houston Astros play here. The stadium also accommodates basketball, conventions, tractor pulls, rodeos and almost any other indoor event. Astrodome seats 66,000 and supplies parking for 30,000 cars. Astrohall is a large exhibition center and Astroarena contains 6,000 theater seats. Call for tickets to events, or to arrange a tour. (713) 799-9500. (p. 26, D–2)

Museum of Natural Science - Aside from dinosaur skeletons and ancient rocks and minerals, the museum contains the Burke Baker Planetarium, The Museum of Medical Science and the Harry C. Weiss Hall of Petroleum Science. 1 Hermann Circle Dr. Daily, call for hours. Admission. (713) 526-4273. (p. 26, D–2)

Anheuser-Busch Brewery - Outlines the brewing process and provides history on the famous brewing family. Visitors of drinking age (21) receive two free samples of the nine brands produced at the brewery. 775 Gellhorn. M-Sa 9-3:30. (713) 670-1695. (p. 26, C–3)

GALVESTON

Famed pirate Jean Laffite set up camp in Galveston in 1817 and rumor has it he buried a treasure beneath Galveston Bay before he was forced to leave the U. S. after "privateering" an American vessel. When Texas became part of the United States, entrepreneurs and investors were attracted to Galveston because of its port and the opportunity to trade cotton and other commodities with Europe. As the city prospered, The Strand, Galveston's business district, became known as "the Wall Street of the Southwest."

A severe hurricane and tidal wave on September 8, 1900 permanently destroyed Galveston's role as an important commercial hub. Still one of the worst natural disasters in U. S. history, the hurricane claimed over 6,000 lives and left an almost totally devastated city. The survivors rallied and over a seven-year period the city was raised six to 17 feet and a 17-foot high, 10-mile long seawall was erected to protect the community being rebuilt inside. Galveston weathered a similar storm in 1915 much better, but faced economic disaster. While Galveston was renovating, Houston widened its narrow ship channel to become Texas' major port. Galveston suffered tremendously from competition with Houston and was never to regain its status as a significant port and commercial hub.

Today Galveston is an engaging family resort with plenty of sun, sea and fresh air. Boating, fishing and beaching are the favorite pastimes of visitors and residents. The Strand, once terribly rundown, has been restored; its impressive ironfront commercial buildings now house shops, boutiques and restaurants. What nature took away from Galveston in terms of a vital shipping industry, she made up for in the natural beauty and recreational opportunities of this lovely seaside community. (*See Galveston city map, p. 27*)

DON'T MISS

Galveston Convention and Visitors Bureau, (409) 763-4311

Treasure Island Tour Train - Hop aboard the open air train for a 90-minute narrated tour of old and new Galveston including historic homes, the Seawall, and downtown. Moody Civic Center, 2106 Seawall. Daily, March-December. Admission. (409) 765-9564. (p. 27, F–8)

The Strand - Historic district where merchandise was brought in from far-away ports. Gas lamps line streets that are dotted with over 100 shops, restaurants and galleries in beautifully restored buildings. Water Street between 20th and 25th. (p. 27, F–8)

The Elissa - The 150-foot square rigged barque is the world's third largest merchant ship afloat. It was christened in 1877 in Aberdeen, Scotland and through 1970 hauled a variety of cargoes to over 150 ports-of-call including Galveston and various ports in Burma, India, Chile and Australia. She still sails at least once a year. Docked on Galveston's main pier. Guided tours available seven days, 9-5. Self-guided tours M-F 10-5, Sa-Su 10-8. Admission. (p. 27, F–8)

Bishop's Palace - This extraordinary home showcases the work of old-time craftsmen. The turreted, rococo exterior and gargoyles were made to order on the premises for Col. Walter Gresham, a Virginia lawyer who fought in the Civil War. The intricate hand-carved woodwork and enormous fireplaces inside have earned it a place on the American Institute of Architecture's list of the country's 100 most architecturally outstanding residential structures, the only residence in Texas with this distinction. 1402 Broadway, M-Sa 10-4, Su 12-4 (winter months 12-4 daily, closed Tuesday all year). Admission. (409) 762-2475. (p. 27, F–8)

The Silk Stocking District - Named for the well-to-do who could afford silk stockings, the district is a nine block area of distinctive homes, some of which are open to the public. The district is loosely bound by N and L Streets along 24th and 25th. Brochures available at the Strand Visitors Center. (p. 27, F–8)

Mary Moody Northern Amphitheater - Alternating evening performances of Broadway favorites and "Lone Star," an epic musical on Texas' struggle for independence which brings history to life. Barbecue dinner after the show. FM 3005 and 13 Mile Road (inside Galveston Island State Park), summer evenings. Admission. (409) 737-1744. (p. 17, C–6)

CORPUS CHRISTI

Corpus Christi is a friendly city whose residents and visitors revel in the beauty of the sun and sea. Alonso Alvarez de Pineda discovered the area while he was mapping out the Gulf Coast in 1519. It was the feast day of Corpus Christi (Body of Christ), so he named the waters after the holiday. The name later carried over to the surrounding land.

Corpus Christi was colonized in 1839 as a supply point for troops stationed further south, where the Mexican War was being fought. When General Zachary Taylor arrived in 1845 to defend Texan territorial claims against the Mexicans, the city flourished and became a classic example of the "Wild West." After the troops departed and the fighting with the Mexicans ceased, Corpus Christi developed into an vibrant deep-water port and prosperous fishing community.

Corpus continues to be the backdrop for a prominent port, the nation's ninth largest. The "Sparkling City by the Sea" benefits greatly from the tourist trade. Corpus Christi's warm climate and almost constant Gulf breezes make it one of Texas' most ideal vacation spots, even in the winter. Fishing excursions are very popular and recreational opportunities abound, including plenty of swimming and boating. Yet the city is not overcrowded and visitors often feel they've tripped upon an undiscovered paradise. The waterfront is peppered with hotels, restaurants and shops that reflect the city's comfortable, informal lifestyle. (*See Corpus Christi city map, p. 23*)

DON'T MISS

Corpus Christi Area Convention & Visitors Bureau, (512) 882-5603

Captain Clark's Flagship - The one hour narrated tour aboard the old-fashioned paddle wheeler explains the port activity and points out the major attractions that are visible on the mainland. Daily departures, times vary with season. Admission. (512) 643-7128. (*p. 23, E–6*)

U. S. Naval Air Station - The Headquarters for Naval Air Training Command where naval officers and aviators receive advance training, this was once the largest naval air station in the world. It features a comprehensive flight line, synthetic training building and an advanced helicopter repair hangar. Tours on Wednesdays at 1, no reservations required. Free. Call (512) 939-2568 for directions. (*p. 23, E–6*)

Museum of Oriental Cultures - A remarkable collection of Chinese and Japanese art including lacquer, cloisonne and models of ancient palaces and shrines. 418 Peoples, Tu-Sa 10-4. Admission. (512) 883-1303. (*p. 23, E–6*)

King Ranch - The largest (823,400 acres) and most famous ranch in the world is located 40 miles from Corpus. Visitors can obtain a pass at the gate and wander around this working ranch to observe ranching and cattle breeding in Texas. Highway 141, Kingsville, TX Su-Fri 10-4. Free admission to ranch, fee for tours. (512) 592-8055. (*p. 19, B–5*)

Padre Island National Seashore - The only national seashore in Texas stretches for 80 miles of the 113-mile long barrier island located between Corpus Christi and Brownsville. Beaching and camping. 9405 South Padre Island Dr, Open daily. Admission. (512) 937-2621 for directions and information. (*p. 19, B–6*)

EL PASO

El Paso is the largest American city directly on the U. S. - Mexican border. El Paso and Juarez are separated only by a small pass of the Rio Grande and are often regarded as one metropolitan area. Through most of its history, the wandering Rio Grande was the official U. S.–Mexican border and with frequent flooding, chunks of land were constantly being traded between the two nations. It wasn't until 1968 that LBJ and Mexican president Gustavo Diaz Ordaz signed an agreement confining the river to a concrete channel, thus establishing a permanent border.

El Paso claims a long, tumultuous history of Mexican, Spanish and Indian raids and revolts. Anglo settlers did not arrive there until the early 19th century. In 1821 when Mexico became independent, El Paso was incorporated as the Mexican city of Chihuahua. Since the city was so far west, it wasn't considered part of Texas when the Republic established itself in 1836. However, 12 years later when the U. S. and Mexico decided to use the Rio Grande as the border, El Paso finally became part of the United States.

El Paso is noted for being closer to San Diego than Houston and closer to the capitals of New Mexico and Arizona than to its own. In fact, El Paso is the only major city on Texas mountain time, so it's one hour earlier there than the rest of the state.

El Paso's economy was buttressed through the late 1840s and 50s by '49ers on their way to the Gold Rush in California. After that, cowboys moving their herds further west contributed to the prosperity of the boom town. The arrival of the railroad guaranteed the city's survival and a more stable community was established with schools, churches, banks and courts.

Today El Paso is a dynamic desert city. The river is a political boundary but residents of El Paso and Juarez still share culture and history. The city's population is 65% Spanish and many residents are bi-lingual. El Paso is a mecca for western wear with many boot and apparel factories cranking out the best of western clothing. The city's economy is largely natural gas, oil refining, agribusiness and copper. Fort Bliss, which began as a campsite for soldiers warding off Apaches, is now the center for all air defense activity for the U. S. Army. The site is larger than Rhode Island and generates over $300 million annually for the local economy. Tourism is also a big business. Visitors are drawn to El Paso's unspoiled desert, high, cool mountains and near-perfect climate. (*See El Paso city map, p. 23*)

DON'T MISS

El Paso Convention and Visitors Bureau, (915) 534-0696

Fort Bliss Museum - Exhibits demonstrate the military role of the fort between 1848-1948 and the role of the missionaries and explorers who settled in El Paso at the turn-of-the-century. Of special interest are the replicas of 19th century forts and historic weapons displays. Located on Fort Bliss, at Pleasant and Pershing, 9-4:30 daily. Free. (915) 568-4518. (*p. 23, E–8*)

Tigua Indian Reservation - This is home to the oldest Indian tribe living in Texas. Visitors can observe their lifestyle, sample their food and visit their adobe homes. 15 miles south of downtown El Paso at 119 S. Old Pueblo Rd. Daily, 11-4:30. Free. (915) 859-3916. (*p. 6, C–2*)

Wilderness Park Museum - Exhibits explore the prehistoric inhabitants of El Paso and their struggle for survival in the desert. Also featured are religious artifacts of the Pueblo Indians. Located in the foothills of the Franklin Mountains, the park offers views of native vegetation and wildlife. 2000 Trans Mountain Road, Tu-Sa 9-5, Free. (915) 755-4332. (*p. 6, C–1*)

The El Paso Museum of Art - For a change of pace from Mexican and Indian art, visit this museum which features a fine permanent collection of the European Masters and American painters. 1211 Montana Ave, Tu-Sa 10-5, Su 1-5. Free. (915) 541-4040. (*p. 23, F–7*)

AMARILLO

Amarillo is the cultural and commercial center of the expansive plains of the Texas Panhandle. The city as we know it might not have existed if not for some mislaid railroad plans. In 1877, the Fort Worth and Denver City Railroad, which was to be constructed diagonally across the Panhandle, strayed from the original survey by about 20 miles southeast, heading straight for another railroad which was being constructed in the opposite direction. Rather than rebuild according to the original plan, the tracks intersected and Amarillo was born. It is unclear whether Amarillo, which means yellow in Spanish, was named for the yellowish creek that ran through the city or the yellow subsoil of the flowering plains.

In no time, Amarillo became one of the country's great cattle shipping markets. At times, over 50,000 head could be seen waiting for transport. For many years no other industry existed, but by the early 1900s, farming began and Amarillo became a major supplier of wheat, grain, cotton and sunflower seeds. In 1918 and 1921 natural gas and petroleum were discovered in the area. Since then, scientists have learned how to extract helium from natural gas and Amarillo has become the "Helium Capital" of the world, supplying an astounding 90 percent of the world's helium.

Despite the presence of large, energy-related corporations, the city maintains the ambiance of a small Western town. Cowboys and ranchers participate in the weekly livestock auction and occasional rodeo. Amarillo has its share of high culture with several fine restaurants and a symphony. (*See Amarillo city map, p. 23*)

DON'T MISS

Amarillo Convention and Visitors Council, (806) 374-1497

The Helium Monument - Was dedicated in 1968 and commemorates the 100th anniversary of the discovery of helium. The most unique feature of the monument is an above-ground time capsule containing over 4,000 items. Located just outside the Don Harrington Discovery Center at 1200 Streit Drive. (*p. 23, B–5*)

Panhandle - Plains Historical Museum - Houses exhibits depicting the pioneer days in West Texas and the Panhandle. US 87 and Fourth Avenue, M-Sa 9-5, Su 2-6. Free. (806) 656-2244. (*p. 4, C–3*)

Cadillac Ranch - This is where eccentric millionaire/pop-artist Stanley Marsh III planted ten vintage Cadillacs in a row with their fin tails in the air— probably the most famous attraction in Amarillo. I-40 W. between Soncy and Helium. (*p. 4, B–3*)

MAJOR LEAGUE SPORTS

BASEBALL

HOUSTON ASTROS
Home games played at
The Astrodome (*p. 26, D–2*),
Kirby Dr. at South Loop 610.
Tickets (713) 526-1709.

TEXAS RANGERS
Home games played at
Arlington Stadium (*p. 24, D–4*),
1700 Copeland Road,
(817) 273-5100.

BASKETBALL

HOUSTON ROCKETS
Home games played at
The Summit (*p. 26, D–2*),
10 Greenway Plaza.
Tickets (713) 627-0600.

DALLAS MAVERICKS
Home games played at
Reunion Arena (*p. 25, D–7*),
777 Sports Street
Tickets (214) 658-7068.

SAN ANTONIO SPURS
Home games played at
Convention Center Arena (*p. 29, D–6*),
South Alamo and Market Streets.
Tickets (512) 554-7773.

FOOTBALL

HOUSTON OILERS
Home games played at
The Astrodome (*p. 26, D–2*),
Kirby Drive at South Loop.
Tickets (713) 797-1000.

DALLAS COWBOYS
Home games played at
Texas Stadium (*p. 25, C–6*),
2401 E. Airport Freeway, Irving.
Tickets (214) 556-9000.

HALF ★ PINT ★ TEXAS

Listed below are special attractions that you may want to treat the kids to if they've had their fill of museums, historic homes and battle sites.

EAST TEXAS/ PINEY WOODS

Astroworld Houston (713) 799-1234. Seventy-five acre park that is part of the Astrodomain complex. "Enchanted Kingdom" provides participatory activities for younger children while the rest of the park has plenty of exciting amusements for older children and adults. (p. 26, D–2)

Battleship "Texas," La Porte, (713) 479-2411. A relic of both world wars, this heavily armed battleship has been moored here since 1948.(p. 27, A–5)

Bluebell Creameries, Brenham, 1-800-327-8135. Weekday tours of the factory that produces what most Texans consider the best ice cream in the world. Everyone will love the samples given out at the end of the tour. (p. 16, B–4)

Merry Christmas Tree Farm, Tomball, 713-351-0818. Forty-two acre farm with over 25,000 trees from which kids can choose between Thanksgiving and Christmas. (p. 17, B–5)

Miniature Horse Farm at the Monastary of St. Clare, Brenham, (409) 836-9652. Cloistered order supports itself almost entirely on the breeding, training and selling of 15 to 34 inch miniature horses. Kids will delight in seeing new foals in the spring. Tours 2-4 Daily. (p. 16, B–4)

CENTRAL TEXAS/ HILL COUNTRY

Austin Children's Museum, Austin, (512) 472-2494. A series of permanent and changing hands-on exhibits especially for children. (p. 22, E–3)

Discovery Hall, Austin, (512) 474-7616. Special science museum geared towards children invites their participation in exhibits. Educational and fun! (p. 22, E–3)

Kiddie Park, San Antonio, (215) 824-4351. Kid-sized merry-go-round and roller coaster. Picnicking facilities. (p. 29, C–6)

The Schlitterbahn, New Braunfels, (512) 625-2351. Large water amusement park also features picnicking facilities, miniature golf and restaurants. (p. 15, C–7)

NORTH CENTRAL TEXAS/ THE "METROPLEX"

Ice Capades Chalet, Galleria Mall, Dallas, (214) 387-5533. One of the rare opportunities in the state for winter sports enthusiasts of all ages. Rentals. (p. 25, B–7)

Kathy Burks Marionettes, Dallas, (214) 353-9277. Puppet and marionette shows featuring over 100 characters from classic fairy tales and children's stories as well as original, modern productions. Call for touring schedule. (p. 25, C–6)

Rainbow Park, Mesquite, (214) 289-5403. Indoor amusement park for kids under 12. (p. 25, D–8)

Ripley's Believe It Or Not! Museum, Grand Prairie, (214) 263-2391. Robert Ripley's collection of thousands of oddities from around the world. Special effects gallery lets visitors experience a simulated tornado and earthquake. (p. 25, D–5)

Telephone Pioneer Museum of Texas, Dallas, (214) 464-4359. Tours and exhibits illustrate the history and future of telecommunications. Geared towards children. (p. 27, D–7)

Texas Safari Ranch, Clifton, (817) 772-7553. World's largest exotic animal drive-through park with over 3,000 animals in 70 species. Kids will love the special petting zoo. (p. 10, D–2)

The Wax Museum of the Southwest, Arlington, (214) 263-2391. Waxen heros of film, the Wild West and American history are on display. "America's Road to Freedom" exhibit features 54 people who were instrumental in shaping America. Also on display is a large collection of antique guns once toted by Western outlaws. (p. 24, D–4)

Wet n' Wild, Arlington, (817) 265-3356. Large water theme park featuring the "Kamikaze Water slide" and the "Corkscrew Flume." Another Wet n' Wild is located in Garland, (214) 271-5637. (p. 24, D–4)

SOUTH TEXAS/ GULF COAST

Jeremiah's Landing, South Padre Island, (512) 761-2131. Water slide, miniature golf, video game arcade. (p. 19, D–7)

Seawolf Park, Galveston, (409) 744-5738. Extensive children's playground, fishing and observation tower overlooking Galveston's Ship Channel. (p. 27, E–8)

THE PANHANDLE

Family Fun Park, Plainview, (806) 293-7902. Water slide, bumper boats, kiddie rides and game room. (p. 4, D–4)

Funland Amusement Park, Wichita Falls, (817) 767-7911. Amusements are small, safe and especially designed for young children. Arcade, miniature golf. (p. 28, F–3)

Storyland Zoo, Amarillo, (806) 378-3000 Ext. 2308. Petting zoo featuring small animals and a fairy tale theme park. (p. 23, B–5)

WEST TEXAS

Insights - El Paso Science Museum, El Paso, (915) 542-2990. Over 80 entertaining hands-on exhibits teaching children about gravity, electricity and the wonders of nature. (p. 23, F–7)

Joyland Amusement Park, (806) 763-2719. Twenty-five rides for toddlers through adolescents. (p. 28, B–2)

Water Wonderland, Midland, (915) 563-3141. Twenty-five acres of water-oriented amusements. Driving range, miniature golf, video arcade. (p. 7, C–8)

The Great Outdoors

Texas has an extensive park system featuring over 100 State Parks, State Recreation Areas, State Historical Parks and State Historical Sites. Many of the State Historical Parks and Sites have been covered in other sections so this section is devoted to the outdoor State Parks and Recreation Areas.

Most parks are open every day, all year. Most allow overnight visitors but close to day visitors by 10 p.m. Parks that are designated as day use only are indicated as such in the descriptions below. Most parks charge small entrance fees and facility fees depending on which facilities are utilized.

Reservations are strongly recommended for overnight facilities, especially during the summer. The maximum advance reservation permitted for campsites, cabins or screened shelters is 90 days. Reservations can be made by calling or writing the park. Most parks also have group facilities and offer annual permits at a discount. For more information on fee schedules, contact the Texas Parks and Wildlife Department, Austin Headquarters, 4200 Smith School Road, Austin, TX 78744. (512) 389-4890.

Please note that the listing below assumes that each area provides rest rooms, showers and picnic areas unless otherwise noted. Also, "waterskiing" indicates that the sport is permitted but facilities are not provided.

EAST TEXAS/ PINEY WOODS

Caddo Lake State Park Rt. 2, Box 15, Karnack, TX 75661, (214) 679-3351. 488 acres on 32,5000 acre Caddo Lake with 40 miles of "boat roads" through intricate channels and bayous. Camping, RV facilities, cabins, hiking trails, boat ramp and rentals, waterskiing. (p. 11, B–7)

Cassells Boykin State Recreational Area c/o Martin Dies Jr. State Park, Rt. 4, Box 274, Jasper, TX 75951, (409) 384-5231. Piney Woods location provides 265 acres on Lake Sam Rayburn with horse rentals and trails. Camping, no showers, boat ramp, fishing, swimming, waterskiing. (p. 11, D–7)

Fairfield Lake State Park Rt. 2, Box 912, Fairfield, TX 75840, (214) 389-4514. 1,460 acres on the shores of 2,350 acre Fairfield Lake. Camping, RV facilities, hiking trails, boat ramp, fishing, swimming waterskiing. (p. 10, D–4)

Lake Bob Sandlin State Park Rt. 5, Box 224, Pittsburgh, TX 75686, (214) 572-5531. Largest lake in the area with a highly developed commercial shoreline. Camping, RV facilities, cabins, hiking trails, boat ramp, fishing, swimming, waterskiing. (p. 11, B–6)

Rusk/Palestine State Park Rt, 4, Box 431, Rusk, TX 75785, (214) 683-5126. The 136 acre Piney Woods location houses the Texas State Railroad Historical Park in which turn-of-the-century steam locomotives pull restored passenger cars along the 25-mile route between Rusk and Palestine. Stocked 15 acre lake, camping, RV facilities, fishing, boat rentals. (p. 11, D–6)

Tyler State Park Rt. 29, Box 29030, Tyler, TX 75706, (214) 597-5338. 985 acres including a trout-stocked spring-fed lake. Camping, RV facilities, boat ramp and rentals, fishing, swimming, hiking trails. (p. 11, C–5)

CENTRAL TEXAS/ HILL COUNTRY

Bastrop State Park Highway 21E. Box 518, Bastrop, TX 78602, (512) 321-2101. Features 3,507 acres of parkland shaded by the "Lost Pines" that strayed far from the Piney Woods of East Texas. Camping, RV facilities, cabins, fishing, hiking trails, pool, golf, scenic drives. (p. 16, B–3)

Colorado Bend State Park Box 108, Bend, TX 76824, (915) 628-3240. 5,328 acres of lush surroundings and waterfalls. Only 300 vehicles permitted inside. Primitive camping, no showers, hiking trails, fishing, swimming. (p. 15, A–6)

Enchanted Rock State Natural Area Rt. 4, Box 170, Fredericksburg, TX 78624, (915) 247-3903. 70 acre dome of pink granite 325 feet high, a geological wonder that is over one billion years old. Indians believed the rock had magical powers. Access to park on foot only. Primitive camping, hiking trails. (p. 15, B–6)

Garner State Park Rt. 70, Box 599, Concan, TX 78838, (512) 232-6132. Central Hill Country location provides 1,420 acres along the cypress-lined Frio River. Camping, RV facilities, cabins, hiking trails, fishing, swimming, boat rentals, miniature golf. (p. 15, C–5)

Guadalupe River State Park HC 54, Box 2087, Bulverde, TX 78163, (512) 438-2656. 1,900 acres along the Guadalupe River with natural rapids and limestone bluffs. Camping, RV facilities, fishing, swimming, hiking trails. (p. 15, C–6)

Hill Country State Natural Area Rt. 1, Box 601, Bandera, TX 78003, (512) 796-6976. 5,370 acres of countryside for hiking and horseback riding. Primitive camping, no showers or restrooms, hiking trails, equestrian area. (p. 15, C–5)

Longhorn Cavern State Park Rt. 2, Box 23, Burnet, TX 78611, (512) 756-4680. 639 acres in the heart of the Hill Country whose highlight is the 11 mile cavern, the world's third largest. 90–minute tour highlights the cavern. Days only, museum. (p. 15, B–7)

Lost Maples State Natural Area HC01, Box 156, Vanderpool, TX 78885, (512) 966-3413. 1,275 acres of bigtooth maple trees and other rare flora and fauna. Optimal time to visit is late October or early November during the peak of foliage season. Camping, RV facilities, museum, hiking trails, fishing, swimming. (p. 15, C–5)

SOUTH TEXAS/ GULF COAST

Choke Canyon State Park Box 2, Calliham, TX 78007, (512) 786-3868. 1,100 acres noted for its diverse wildlife (westernmost home of the American alligator). Camping, RV facilities, hiking trails, museum, pool, swimming, fishing, boat ramp and rentals, waterskiing. (p. 16, D–1)

Falcon State Recreational Area Box 2, Falcon Heights, TX 78545, (512) 848-5327. 572 acres on the eastern shore of the 87,000 acre Falcon Reservoir. Excellent birdwatching, international crossing into Mexico via the Falcon dam. Camping, RV facilities, boat ramp, fishing, swimming, waterskiing. (p. 18, C–4)

Galveston Island State Park Rt. 1, Box 156A, Galveston, TX 77554, (409) 737-1222. 1,944 acres between the Gulf beaches and Galveston Bay. Special attraction is the summer performances of "The Lone Star" and Broadway shows. Camping, RV facilities, hiking trails, fishing, swimming. (p. 17, C–6)

Lake Corpus Christi State Recreational Area Box 1167, Mathis, TX 78368, (512) 547-2635. 365 acres on the southern edge of the 27 mile-long lake. Camping, RV facilities, boat ramp and rentals, fishing, swimming, waterskiing. (p. 19, A–5)

Matagorda Island State Park Box 117, Port O'Connor, TX 77982, (512) 983-2215. 7,325 acres and is known for its rustic, primitive camping. No RV hookups or showers, fishing, swimming, waterskiing. (p. 19, A–8)

Mustang Island State Park Box 326, Port Aransas, TX 78373, (512) 749-5246. 3,704 acres on the island between Corpus Christi Bay and the Gulf of Mexico where wild mustangs once roamed free along the 5 miles of Gulf beach frontage. Camping, RV facilities, fishing, swimming. (p. 19, B–7)

Sea Rim State Park Box 1066, Sabine Pass, TX 77655, (409) 971-2559. 15,109 acres of beach and marshland that is ideal for birdwatching. Camping, fishing, swimming, boat ramp, museum, hiking trails. (p. 17, B–8)

NORTH TEXAS/ METROPLEX AREA

Bonham State Recreational Area Rt. 1, Box 337, Bonham, TX 75418, (214) 583-5022. 261 heavily wooded acres including a lake with a lighted fishing pier. Camping, RV facilities, boat ramp and rentals, fishing, swimming. (p. 10, A–4)

Dinosaur Valley State Park Box 396, Glen Rose, TX 76043, (817) 897-4588. 1,272 acres; don't miss the dinosaur footprints that were left over 100 million years ago. Camping, RV facilities, Texas longhorn herd, hiking trails, equestrian area, fishing and swimming in Paluxy River. (p. 10, C–2)

PANHANDLE

Abilene State Park Rt. 1, Tuscola, TX 79562, (915) 572-3204. Provides 621 acres including a natural spring swimming pool and Texas Longhorn herd. Lake Abilene is adjacent. Camping, RV facilities, pool, swimming, hiking trails. (p. 8, C–4)

Big Spring State Recreational Area Box 1064, Big Spring, TX 79720, (915) 263-4913. 370 acres especially known for its 200 foot mesa and scenic drives. Day use only. Museum, hiking trail. (p. 8, C–2)

Caprock Canyons State Park Box 204, Quitaque, TX 79255, (806) 455-1492. 13,566 acres including two man-made lakes. Imported African wildlife inhabits the park. Horseback riding facilities and 5,000 acres for trail riding. Camping, RV facilities, hiking trails, equestrian area, boat ramp, fishing, swimming, museums. (p. 5, C–5)

Lake Arrowhead State Recreational Area Rt. 2, Box 260, Wichita Falls, TX 76301, (817) 528-2211. 524 acres on the shores of Lake Arrowhead are known for great fishing. Camping, RV facilities, equestrian area, boat ramp, swimming, fishing, waterskiing. (p. 10, A–1)

Mackenzie State Recreational Area Parks and Recreation Director, City Hall, Lubbock, TX 79408, (806) 767-2660. More widely visited than any other state recreational area in Texas, the 542 acres include Prairie Dog Town, one of the few remaining colonies of the mischievous rodents. Day use only. No showers, pool, golf. (p. 8, A–1)

Palo Duro Canyon State Park Rt. 2, Box 285, Canyon, TX 79015, (806) 488-2227. Location provides 16,402 acres centering on the dramatic canyon that is over 1,000 feet deep and 100 miles long, illustrating the area's ancient geological history. Longhorn herd. Camping, RV facilities, equestrian area, horse rentals, scenic drive, museum, hiking trails. "Texas" epic performed on summer evenings. (p. 4, C–4)

Possum Kingdom State Recreational Area Box 36, Caddo, TX 76029, (817) 549-1803. Location features 1,529 acres on Possum Kingdom Lake. Special features include scuba diving (up to 150 feet) and a Texas Longhorn herd. Camping, RV facilities, cabins, boat ramp and rentals, fishing, swimming, waterskiing. (p. 9, B–6)

WEST TEXAS

Balmorhea State Park Box 15, Toyahvale, TX 79786, (915) 375-2370. 46 acre area especially noted for containing the San Solomon spring-fed pool, the world's largest. Camping, RV facilities, swimming, lodging. (p. 13, B–5)

Davis Mountains State Park Box 786, Ft. Davis, TX 79734, (915) 426-3337. Location features 1,896 acres of desert and woodlands in the Davis Mountains. Special feature is Indian Lodge, a pueblo-style hotel built by the Civilian Conservation Corps in the 1930's. Camping, RV facilities, museum, hiking trails, scenic drive. (p. 13, B–5)

Monahans Sandhills State Park Box 1738, Monahans, TX 79756, (915) 943-2092. 3,840 acres consisting of constantly shifting wind sculpted sand dunes. Museum highlights historical, archeological and biological features of the "Texas Sahara". Camping, RV facilities, hiking trails. (p. 7, C–7)

WEST TEXAS also contains the state's two National Parks:

Big Bend National Park TX, 79834, (915) 477-2251. Spectacular 775,240 acres in West Texas where the Rio Grand bends north before turning south again. The largest park in Texas, its fantastic assets include the Rio Grande, the Chihuahan Desert, and the Chisos Mountains. Exhibits, guided tours, hiking trails, camping, RV facilities, horseback riding, rafting, boating, fishing. Lodging available. (p. 13, D–5)

Guadalupe Mountains National Park HC60, Box 400, Fault Flat, TX 79847. 79,293 acres of scenic, rugged terrain including four of Texas' highest peaks. The highest, Guadalupe Peak, reaches 8,749 feet into the sky. Exhibits, guided tours, hiking, camping, no RV hookups. (p. 6, C–4)

TOURS

SCENIC DRIVES

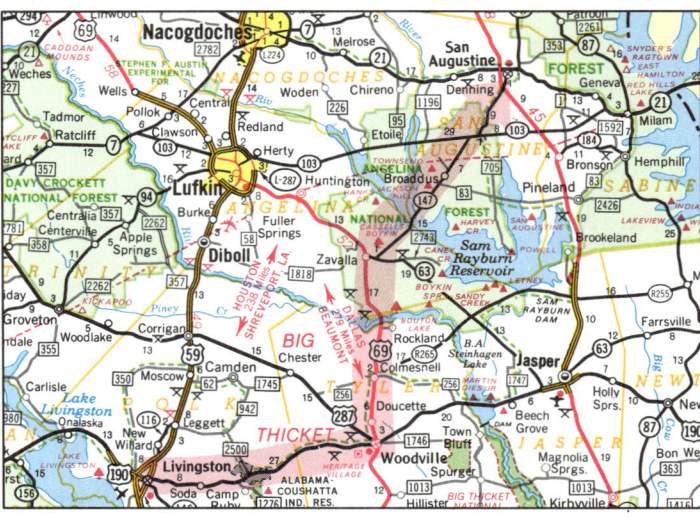

EAST TEXAS / Livingston to San Augustine

A heavily forested trip through the Piney Woods of Texas with plenty of fishing, boating, hiking and camping available for travelers. The Alabama - Coushatta Indian Reservation and the Heritage Garden, both West of Woodville, make great side trips. This drive is especially scenic in the spring when the dogwood trees and wildflowers are in bloom. (*Approximately 95 miles*)

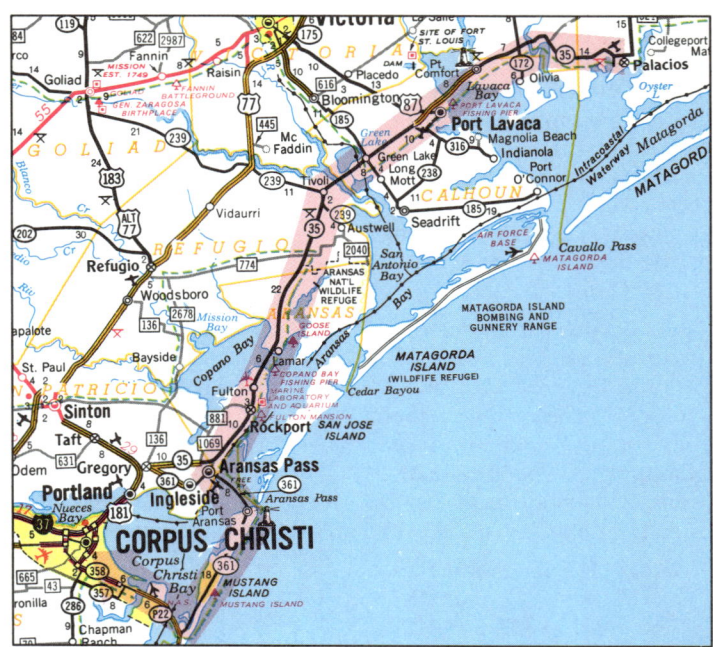

TEXAS COAST / Palacios to Corpus Christi

Fishing, both commercial and sport, are major industries in this area. Charter services are available for offshore fishing. Aransas National Wildlife Refuge is the winter home of the whooping crane. Mustang Island is one of the most popular beach areas in Texas. Good accommodations are available all along this route. (*Approximately 132 miles*)

TEXAS RIO GRANDE VALLEY / Brownsville to McAllen

Palms and citrus trees line the highways along this route. A major fruit and vegetable growing area, tourism also is a major segment of the economy. In Brownsville, it's simple to cross the border into Mexico for a day's shopping. In McAllen, visit the Santa-Ana National Wildlife Refuge and the McAllen International Museum. The Mexican border towns of Matamoros and Reymosa are colorful and feature fine restaurants and excellent shopping.
(Approximately 55 miles)

WEST TEXAS / Alpine to Kent

This rugged mountain area offers spectacular vistas, camping, swimming and mountain climbing. Visit historic Ft. Davis operated by the National Park Service; it has been restored and offers comprehensive history and nature programs in the summer. Davis Mountains State Park has excellent camping facilities and the McDonald Observatory on Mt. Locke has tours for the general public.
(Approximately 76 miles)

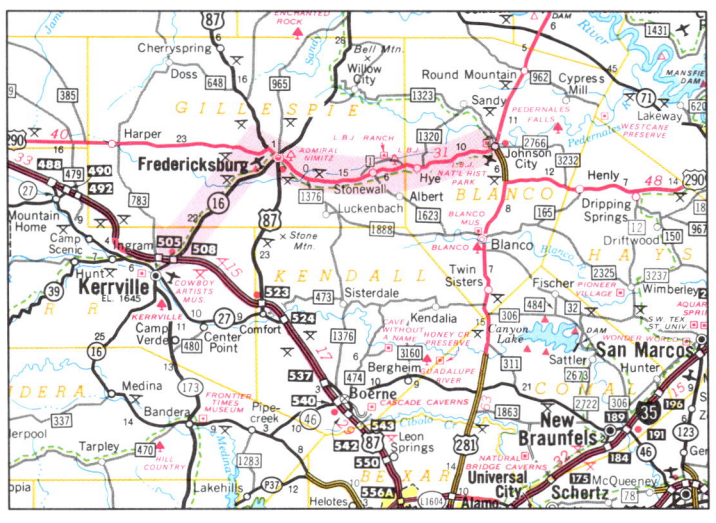

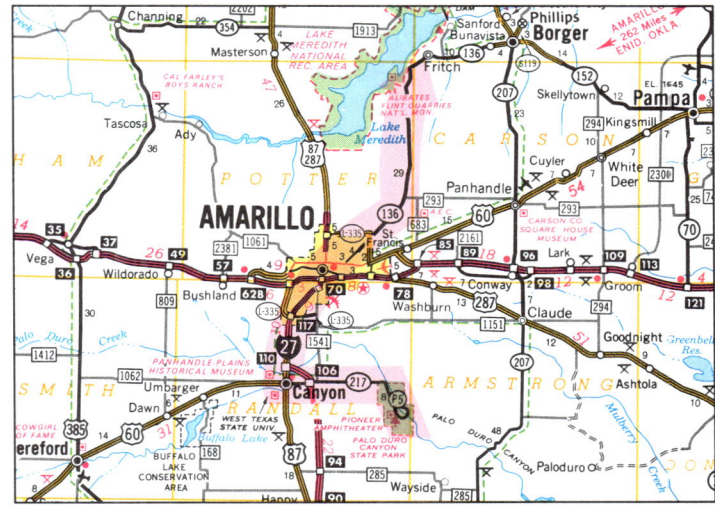

TEXAS HILL COUNTRY / Johnson City to Kerrville

This area of Texas is known for its beautiful hills, delightful climate and outdoor recreational opportunities. In Johnson City, visit the boyhood home of President Lyndon Baines Johnson and at Stonewall, famous for its delicious peaches, the LBJ Ranch. Fredericksburg, birthplace of Admiral Chester Nimitz, was settled by Germans in the mid 1800's. The Admiral Nimitz State Historical Site and many of the early homes and buildings have been restored. "Night in Old Fredericksburg" and "Oktoberfest" are annual events. In Kerrville, visit the Cowboy Artists of America Museum.
(Approximately 55 miles)

THE PANHANDLE / Palo Duro Canyon State Park to Fritch

Palo Duro Canyon, the largest of all Texas parks boasts colorful vistas, hiking trails, camping, horseback riding and miniature train rides. The amphitheater presents "Texas," an outdoor drama in the summer. In Canyon, visit the Panhandle Plains Museum and in Amarillo, the Dan Harrington Discovery Center. The Alibates Flint Quarries National Monument on the south shore of Lake Meredith was prized by the Indians. Lake Meredith Recreation Area has fishing, swimming, boating, waterskiing and camping.
(Approximately 75 miles)

SURPRISE

TEXAS WINERIES

Wine connoisseurs and laymen alike are surprised to discover that the Lone Star State boasts 25 commercial wineries with over 7,000 acres under cultivation. They are further fascinated by the fact that winemaking in Texas is not new but is the renaissance of a lost craft that was started 100 years before the first vine was ever planted in Napa Valley.

The first vintors in Texas were the Franciscan Friars who settled in El Paso and by 1662 were busy making sacramental wines. The business of winemaking spread beyond the clergy and the confines of West Texas and by the early 20th century there were 25 wineries in the state. Prohibition put all but one of the vineyards out of business and only the Val Verde, which was founded in 1883, was operational in the early 1970s.

In the mid-70s the University of Texas and Texas A&M launched an ambitious viticultural research program and determined that premium grape growing conditions existed in several regions of the state. The studies found that with long growing seasons, early springs and high sunlight intensity, wine grapes prosper. Armed with this documentation and plenty of patience and hope, would-be vintors began planting and tending irrigated vineyards from the Panhandle to the Piney Woods. Experts from both in and outside the state have described the industry's growth as "explosive" and "spectacular," claims which are bolstered by the fact that in 1982, 50,000 gallons of wine were produced in Texas and by 1988, the figure had jumped to 750,000 gallons.

Comparatively, winemaking in Texas is still in its infancy but wine aficionados all over the world are beginning to take notice as several Texas wineries have walked away from national and international competitions with gold and silver medals. The International Wine Expo and the Lone Star Wine Competition (both held in Dallas) attract the greatest number of Texan contestants and their showings are improving as their vines mature and produce quality whites, reds and champagnes.

Fine restaurants and stores around the country now feature Texas wines but it's even better to try one at a Lone Star winery. They are located in all regions of the state and most offer tours and tastings. Before you visit, give the winery a call to verify hours or make an appointment.

SELECTED TEXAS VINEYARDS

CENTRAL TEXAS/ HILL COUNTRY

Fall Creek Vineyards Box 68, Tow, TX 78672, (512) 476-4477. Sixty-five acres planted for vinifera (European grapes that thrive in warm, dry climates to produce Chardonnay, Cabernet Sauvignon and Riesling). Fall Creek has won awards for its Riesling and its other wines have been served at the White House. Tours and tastings are available on the last Saturday of every month (excluding November and December) from 1-5 p.m. (p. 15, A–6)

Oberhellmann Vineyards HC61, Box 22, Fredericksburg, TX 78130, (512) 685-3297. Founded in 1976, this 40 acre vineyard turns out vinifera including Pinot Noir, Cabernet Sauvignon and Johannisberg Riesling. Tours and tastings are available Saturdays from Easter through Christmas, 10-4 p.m. (p. 15, B–6)

Moyer Texas Champagne Company 1941 IH-35E, New Braunfels, TX 78130, (512) 625-5181. The sparkling wine is produced "methode champenoise" (fermented and bottle aged) and won a medal in the *Dallas Morning News* Wine Competition. Guided tours and tastings Monday-Saturday 10-5 p.m. (p. 16, C–2)

EAST TEXAS/ PINEY WOODS

Messina Hof Wine Cellars Rt. 7, Box 905, Bryan, TX 77802, (409) 778-9463. Thirty-acres of American and Europeans varieties include Chenin Blanc, Muscat Canelli and White Zinfandel. The vineyard has collected over 40 awards for its wines. Guided tours and tastings by appointment only. (p. 16, A–4)

Piney Woods Country Wines 3408 Willow Dr, Orange, TX 77630 (409) 883-5403. This vineyard specializes in fruit-based country wines made from locally grown fruits, berries and grapes. Tours and tastings M-Sa 9-6, Su 12-6. (p. 17, B–8)

NORTH TEXAS/ METROPLEX

La Buena Vida Vineyards Rt. 2, Box 927, Fort Worth, TX 76135, (817) 237-9463. Twelve acres of French-American hybrids produce 20,000 gallons per year of award winning Vintage Port, Rayon D'or, Mist Blush and Vidal Blanc. Tours and tastings M-Sa 11-5 p.m., Sun 12-5 p.m. Reservations recommended. (p. 24, C–1)

Sanchez Creek Vineyard 3501 Old Dennis Rd, Weatherford, TX 76087, (817) 594-6884. One of the few Texas vineyards specializing in red wines, this small winery is named after the creek than runs among the vines. Tours by appointment. (p. 9, B–7)

SOUTH TEXAS

Val Verde Winery 100 Qualia Dr, Del Rio, TX 78840, (512) 775-9714. This 30 acre family run vineyard is the oldest in Texas producing award-winning Tawny Port, Lenoir, Johannisberg Riesling and Cabernet Sauvignon. The winery is housed in a historic adobe building. Tours and tastings upon request M-Sa 9-5 p.m. (*p. 14, C–3*)

PANHANDLE

Llano Estacado Winery FM 1585, Box 3487, Lubbock, TX 79452, (806) 745-2258. One of the state's largest wineries and generally regarded as its most promising, Llano Estacado has won several gold medals at national competitions for their Cabernet Sauvignon and Chardonnay. Guided tours and tastings, M-S 10-4 p.m., Su 12-4 p.m. (*p. 8, A–1*)

Pheasant Ridge Winery Rt. 3, Box 191, Lubbock, TX 79401, (806) 746-6033. Pheasant Ridge is named after the wild birds that are often spotted in the area. The 47 acres are devoted to the vinifera varieties that produce their award winning Cabernet Sauvignon, Chenin Blanc, Chardonnay and Sauvignon Blanc. Tours and tastings by appointment only. (*p. 8, A–1*)

WEST TEXAS

Ste. Genevieve Wines Box 687, Ft. Stockton, TX 79735, (915) 395-2417 or (915) 417-9555. Texas' largest winery with over 1,000 acres and storage for 1.4 million gallons. Owned by a French company. Tours and tastings are by appointment. (*p. 13, B–7*)

Bieganowski Cellars 5923 W. Gateway, El Paso, TX 79925, (915) 775-0842. El Paso was one of the first wine-making areas of the U.S. and today this new winery blends old-world techniques with modern technology. Tours and tastings by appointment. (*p. 23, E–8*)

CROSSING THE BORDER

The allure of Mexico and the ease of traveling to and from border areas augments the attraction of visiting or living in Texas. In many South and West Texas towns, Mexico is only a bridge away and crossing the border makes for an exciting excursion for shopping, dining and nightlife. Border areas are defined as anything within a 75 mile area of the border. U. S. citizens require no visas, passports or other documentation to make the trip as long as they stay within the border area for less than 72 hours. Visits beyond the border area or for a longer duration require a Mexican tourist card which can be obtained from Mexican immigration authorities stationed at the border.

Most people walk across the border but automobiles are also permitted. However, according to Mexican statutes, it is illegal to operate a motor vehicle in Mexico without auto insurance issued by a Mexican insurance company. For that reason, it is recommended that you walk or take a shuttle service as you cross into Mexico, although short-term Mexican auto insurance is available from travel services and insurance agencies located along the Texas side of the border.

U. S. dollars are accepted by nearly all merchants and vendors at the current exchange rate. Mexican banks, hotels and tourist facilities will exchange currency but that will most likely not be necessary. Each U. S. citizen may bring Mexican purchases valued up to $400 retail into the U. S. duty free, upon any one re-entry or once every 30 days. Merchandise over the $400 limit will be assessed federal duty fees. However, there are exemptions on certain jewelry and hand-crafted items. U. S. Customs officials stationed at the border can advise you.

There are, of course, prohibited imports such as narcotics, weapons, fruits, vegetables, plants, animals, birds and items made from the skin, feathers or teeth of endangered species. The U. S. Embassy in Mexico can provide a complete list of prohibited products. Federal law also specifies that each adult can bring only one quart or liter of duty-free alcoholic beverages back into the U. S. each 30 days.

The most common border crossing is into **Nuevo Laredo**, Mexico from Laredo, Texas (*p. 18, B–3*). Over 30 million people traverse the two connecting bridges each year. Most of the residents of Nuevo Laredo speak English and there is plenty of bartering to be done on Guerrero Street. This main drag is lined with shops and boutiques featuring jewelry, hand-made crafts, leather, silver and home furnishings. Bars and restaurants are also interspersed along Guerrero. Nuevo Laredo is especially noted for Nuevo Laredo Downs, a beautiful thoroughbred race track with sophisticated betting equipment and luxury dining facilities.

From El Paso there are three border crossings into **Juarez**, Mexico (*p. 6, C–1*). Once there, take advantage of several shopping venues, the most comprehensive of which is ProNaf. A government sponsored mall-type complex, ProNaf features an array of vendors. However, if you love to bargain, this is not the place to do it since prices are fixed (but reasonable). For bargaining, try the colorful City Market where hand-crafted Mexican items can be had for almost any price. Juarez also has a race track but is noted for the bullfights held on most Sunday evenings at the Plaza de Toros Monumental Bullring.

Matamoros, Mexico is just across the bridge from Brownsville, TX (*p. 19, D–5*) and is the largest Rio Grande Valley city on either side of the border. Tour buses run daily on sightseeing and shopping excursions and are a good way to cover a large area within a short amount of time. Like other border towns, you can spend hours in Matamoros strolling among the shops and restaurants surrounded by street performers, vendors and musicians. You can bargain almost anywhere you go for onyx, crystal, brassware and crafts.

FOOD

Texans are as serious about their chili as they are about politics and oil leases.

HOT! HOT! HOT! HOT!

A Georgia peach is like none other and you could never quite duplicate the cajun shrimp you had at Mardi Gras back in '75. You stock up on Washington apples once they hit the store and that fresh, boiled lobster alone is worth a trip back to Maine. But what about Texas? How do you choose between chili and chicken-fried steak?

Texas is not known for one particular dish or type of produce (like most states), instead it's a unique patchwork of choices based on its history, culture and people (like most countries). "When in Rome..." is good advice and in Texas that could mean Huevos Rancheros for breakfast, fried chicken and okra for lunch, and barbecued hot links for supper. The food in Texas is as broad as the state lines, as diverse as the population and as relished as a Sunday afternoon full of back-to-back football games.

To begin with, there's chili and there's chilie and it's easier to nail grape jelly to a barn door than to find a Texan alive who doesn't know the difference. Chili is the official State Dish and is made by slow-cooking beef, tomatoes and spices, the most crucial of which are chilies, which are peppers. To make things even more confusing, the variations of chili are innumerable. Some folks cut the beef into 1/4" cubes while others prefer it ground; some use lots of tomatoes and some none at all; some even add venison or bourbon. Still others swear by ancho chilies while others wouldn't dream of using anything but jalapenos. There seems to be only one thing that Texans agree on: Real Texans don't add beans (not to mention sour cream or cheese)! While other southwestern states shred their beef or load their chili with kidney or pinto beans, Texans simply don't.

Texans are as serious about their chili as they are about politics and oil leases. "Chiliheads" converge frequently whether it's at a local cook-off or at an annual meeting of the International Chili Society. Bar room historians recall the "Chili Queens" of the turn-of-the-century along Military Plaza in San Antonio, dipping "bowls of red" to the politicians, evangelists, street performers and vagabonds who gathered there after the merchants had vacated their stands and pushcarts for the day. The practice flourished until 1936 when the Board of Health put an end to it because questionable ingredients were being used in the State Dish.

Chili was most likely invented to mask the flavor of poorer cuts of beef and to satisfy the palates of rambunctious cowboys gathered around the chuck wagon. Today Texans get a big kick out of the redundancy of a Yankee who orders chili con carne (which means peppers with meat) or dips his saltines rather than crumbling them into the bowl. Though they differ among themselves about ingredients and realize that no two pots cook the same way, none have patience for the Californians who are compelled to add bell peppers, celery or olives.

If chili is the State Dish then Tex-Mex is the State Cuisine. Tex-Mex developed when Mexican food "crossed the border" and was re-invented for Texans. A good example is the tortilla. A Mexican tortilla is made with corn, which is abundant in interior Mexico, while a tortilla in Texas is generally made with flour as wheat is easier to grow in Texas. The Old Borunda Cafe, which opened in Marfa, Texas in 1887, is credited with being the first Tex-Mex restaurant. There, a Mexican cook adapted traditional Mexican recipes for Texan tastes.

Today, a Tex-Mex plate features flour tortillas in many different guises. An enchilada is a soft tortilla filled with cheese, beef or chicken and topped with a chilie sauce, onion and more cheese. Chilie rellenos are mild peppers stuffed with cheese and other ingredients and deep fried. Fajitas are strips of marinated skirt steaks grilled over mesquite and served in soft tortillas. The list goes on, and though the names of these Tex-Mex favorites are invariably Mexican, the dishes themselves are derivatives of their Mexican predecessors and are quite different from what is served in Mexico. Further, the oral tradition of these recipes account for the diversity of their preparation. Most of Texas' finest cooks are not trained chefs but home cooks who bring rich regional and familial variations to the food.

Though much of the food in Texas borrows heavily from its Hispanic heritage and Southwestern neighbors in the form of Tex-Mex, barbecue is pure Tex. It's been said that "Texas is a place where they barbecue everything but ice cream, even the tires off a Cadillac." Armadillo, venison and rattlesnake all make good eating but most common are brisket, ribs, shoulder and rings of sausage known as hot links. Barbecue began on ranches where entire steers were cooked over mesquite to feed large numbers of hungry ranch hands. The word "barbecue" comes from the Spanish "barbacoa" which refers to the wood that supports the meat over fire. Because it grew fast and was plucked young, mesquite burned hot and became the favorite, but hickory, oak and other dry wood also worked well.

Real Texas barbecue hasn't changed much, and the intoxicating aroma of smoked meats makes mouths water from Abilene to Zapata. The beef cooks for hours, even days, away from the direct heat of the flame. Purists use no sauce and never turn or baste the meat while it's cooking. Restaurants will put their own sauce on the table whether or not it's used in preparation and those recipes are among the best kept secrets in The Lone Star State. Sauce or not, the best barbecue is served with no frills, generally on a piece of red butcher paper, with a slice or two of white bread and maybe some coleslaw and potato salad. It's expected that you'll eat it with your hands and no one cares if you get sauce on your face, lick your fingers or use a whole box of paper napkins.

In December of 1963, LBJ entertained his first foreign visitor since becoming President at the "Texas White House," his ranch in Stonewall. The festivities included a no-holds-barred barbecue in the local high school gymnasium. The First Lady worried that the Chancellor of West Germany would perceive them as unsophisticated until he confided, "Frau Johnson, I feel at home with you." Whether it was the hot links or the hospitality, Texas food has a way of making people feel at home.

"Down home" cooking is another staple of Texas cuisine. It was brought by the Southerners who migrated to East Texas.

Continued on page 53

TEXAS RECIPES

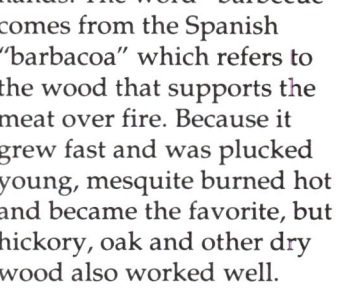

Sour Cream Enchiladas
Tex-Mex
Mike and Charlie's, Austin, TX

Ingredients
6-inch corn tortillas
Grated cheese, 1/2 cheddar and 1/2 Monterey Jack
1/4 lb. butter
1/2 cup flour
1 quart hot half-and-half
5 lbs. sour cream
Salt
Pepper
Tabasco
Cumin
Jalapeno juice
Paprika

Method
Dip tortillas in hot oil to soften. Roll up with grated cheese. Cover with sauce, garnish with cheese and paprika.

For the sauce, make a roux with butter and flour, adding the hot half-and-half sour cream. Season to taste with salt and pepper, Tabasco, cumin and jalapeno juice. Bake at 350 degrees for 5 to 10 minutes in conventional oven or in microwave for 45 seconds.

Chicken–Fried Steak
Southern/Country
Y–O Ranch, Mountain Home, TX

Ingredients
6 - 7 oz. portions of tenderized beef
Salt and pepper to taste
5 eggs
1 12-oz. can evaporated milk
2–3 cups shortening or oil
Flour for dredging plus 3 Tbsp. all purpose flour
2 cups water

Method
Sprinkle meat with salt and pepper, set aside. Beat the eggs and one half cup of milk together. Heat oil in heavy deep-sided skillet to temperature of 350 degrees. Dredge the steaks with flour, dip them in the batter, then in flour again. When oil is hot, add steaks a few at a time. Fry for 4 minutes on one side or until golden brown, then do other side. Drain on paper towels. For the gravy, pour all but 4 Tbsp. of the fat from the skillet and turn the heat to low, add 3 Tbsp. of flour and cook over low heat, stirring constantly for 3 minutes. Do not burn. Add the remaining milk, whisking until smooth. Then add the water gradually, stirring constantly until the gravy is smooth and of desired thickness. Add salt and pepper to taste. Serve steaks with sauce on the side.

Texas Prime Rib
Barbecue
Kreuz Market, Lockhurt, TX

Ingredients
6 lbs Texas Prime
Salt to taste
Post oak (for cooking flavor)
35-foot chimney

Method
Place meat at indirect heat source for 8-10 hours, rotate every 25 minutes.

Annual Fairs & Festivals

Texans are more than happy to celebrate almost any thing: history, holidays, crops, food (especially the hotter and more exotic varieties), animals, even insects. What follows is a selection of Texas' most unusual and renowned events. For a more complete events calendar, contact the Tourism Division of the Texas Department of Commerce, P.O. Box 12008, Austin, Texas 78711.

JANUARY

Great Country River Festival (*San Antonio*) Country and western music festival where various bands play from barges and stages set up in and along the San Antonio River and the River Walk. Held one weekend in late January. Call (512) 227-4262 for information or contact radio station KKYX in **San Antonio**.

New Year's Day Cotton Bowl Parade and Game (*Dallas*) The traditional New Year's Day match-up between the Southwest Conference champion and a nationally ranked guest is a football classic. Just as famous is the nationally-televised parade preceding the game. Mobil Cotton Bowl Classic, P.O. Box 569420, **Dallas**, TX, 75356, (214) 634-7525.

Southwestern Exposition and Fat Stock Show and Rodeo (*Fort Worth*) Over 90 years old, this nationally acclaimed expo is the biggest annual event in Fort Worth. Over 15,000 head of livestock are judged during the show and top cowboys and famous entertainers perform. Parade, livestock auctions, commercial exhibits and carnivals. Generally held 17 days in late January through early February. Southwestern Exposition Stock Show, P.O. Box 150, **Fort Worth**, TX 76101. (817) 877-2400.

Texas Citrus Fiesta (*Mission*) Since 1932 the Rio Grande Valley has paid homage to the citrus industry in Texas with a number of unusual events including the Parade of Oranges, the Coronation of Queen Citrianna and King Citrus. Generally held for two weeks near the end of January. Texas Citrus Fiesta, P.O. Box 407, **Mission**, TX 78572, (512) 585-9724, or contact Mission Chamber of Commerce at (512) 585-2727.

FEBRUARY

Charro Days (*Brownsville, TX - Matamoros, Mexico*) The weeklong fiesta in late February has been celebrated since 1938 and honors the charro horseman of Mexico who possessed outstanding riding skills. Events on both sides of the border include parades, fiestas, street dances, carnival acts and floor shows with many of the participants in traditional Mexican dress. Generally held for a long weekend in mid-to-late February. Contact the Brownsville Visitor's Center (800) 626-2639.

George Washington's Birthday Celebration (*Laredo*) Nobody knows why George's birthday has been celebrated in such grand style here since 1898. Laredo and its sister-city Nuevo Laredo across the border hold a 10-day fiesta each February including fireworks, parades, a Jalapeno festival and mariachi music. Washington's Birthday Celebration Association, P.O., Box 816, **Laredo**, TX 78042-0816, (512) 722-0589.

Houston Livestock Show and Rodeo (*Houston*) 14 days of rodeo and livestock competition with top-name country and western entertainment attract exhibitors and spectators from all over the state for the largest stock show and second largest rodeo in the nation. Mid-February for two weeks. Houston Livestock Show and Rodeo, P. O. Box 20070, **Houston**, TX 77225, (713) 791-9000.

Mardi Gras (*Galveston*) Look out, New Orleans! The ten days preceding Ash Wednesday are packed with parades, festivals, costume contests and entertainment. The Saturday night before Ash Wednesday is the Momus Grand Night Parade featuring a procession of jazz musicians and spectacular floats. Galveston Island Convention & Visitors Bureau, 2106 Seawall Boulevard, **Galveston**, TX 77550, (409) 763-4311.

MARCH

Azalea and Spring Flower Trial (*Tyler*) A seven-mile trail winds through residential gardens revealing a plethora of spring flowers and brilliant colors. Guided tours are available of four homes in the historic area and horse-drawn carriages provide elegant rides through the redolent Azalea District. Date for the Trail varies with the estimated "peak" of the blooming flowers. Chamber of Commerce, P.O. Box 390, **Tyler**, TX 75710, (214) 592-1661.

Houston International Festival (*Houston*) One of the greatest indoor/outdoor celebrations of the performing and visual arts in the country featuring local, national and international talent. Houston International Festival, 909 Fannin St., Suite P330, **Houston**, TX 77010, (713) 654-8808.

Texas Dogwood Trails Festival (*Palestine*) Though the Festival's accompanying activities include rodeos, parades, air shows, square dancing and sports, the highlights are the blossoming trees and flowers along a five-mile route in Davey Dogwood Park and the rural Palestine roads. Festival is held weekends only late March through early April. Dogwood Trails, 400 North Queen St, **Palestine**, TX 75801, (214) 729-7275.

Texas Independence Day Celebration (*Washington*) Historic reenactments with period attire and military displays at the site of the signing of the Texas Declaration of Independence (signed March 2, 1836). Generally held first weekend in March. Washington-on-the-Brazos State Park, Box 305, **Washington**, TX 77880, (409) 878-2214.

Shakespeare Festival (*Odessa*) The Bard's works are presented Thursday-Saturday throughout March and April in a replica of the original 16th-century Globe Theatre. Globe Theatre, 2308 Shakespeare Road, **Odessa**, TX 79761, (915) 332-1586.

Sweetwater Jaycees Rattlesnake Roundup (*Sweetwater*) The world's largest Rattlesnake Roundup began in 1958 when the Jaycees decided to help the ranchers and farmers plagued by rattlers. What started out as a hunt has evolved into a festival and seven to eight *tons* of rattlesnake are captured each year. For spectators there are snake-handling demonstrations, rattlesnake eating contests, road races and dances. For hunters, the registration fee includes an insurance policy! Generally held the second weekend in March, Chamber of Commerce, P.O. Box 1148, **Sweetwater**, TX 79556, (915) 235-5488.

APRIL

Buccaneer Days (*Corpus Christi*) This annual 10-day festival has gone on for over 50 years and celebrates the history of the coastal area and the 1519 discovery of Corpus Christi Bay. Water-oriented events include sailboat regattas, fishing tournaments, carnival, parade, biathlon and spectacular fireworks displays. Buccaneer Commission, Inc., P.O. Box 30404, **Corpus Christi**, TX 78404, (512) 882-3242.

Derrick Days (*Corsicana*) City-wide festival celebrates the discovery of oil and the heritage of Corsicana, site of the first oil field west of the Mississippi and a boom town in the 1890's. Events include exhibits at the Oil and Energy Museum, chili cook-off, regatta and a barn dance. Derrick Days, Box 622, **Corsicana**, TX 75151, (214) 872-3931.

Fiesta (*San Antonio*) For 10 days in April the entire city celebrates a fiesta that has been likened to Mardi Gras in New Orleans. Concerts, costumed dancers, parades, floats and balls with a Mexican flair culminate in Night in Old San Antonio. The four night spectacular reenacts early San Antonio fiestas and features plenty of ethnic foods, traditional music and a charreada (Mexican Rodeo). Fiesta San Antonio Commission, 1145 East Commerce, **San Antonio**, TX 78205, (512) 227-5191.

Highland Lakes Bluebonnet Trail (*Austin and vicinity*) The trail route is covered with native wildflowers including bluebonnets (the state flower), yuccas and Indian paintbrush among others. Arts and crafts displays, sports competitions and food concessions. Generally held for two weekends in mid-April. Highland Lakes Tourist Assoc. P.O. Box 13371, **Austin**, TX 78711-3371, (512) 793-6666.

Legends of Golf Tournament (*Austin*) Some of the greatest golf veterans (age 50 and over) compete in what is regarded as the best "old-timers" tourney in the game. Usually held the third weekend in April. Legends of Golf, 1120 Capital of Texas Highway, Building 2, Suite 300, Austin, TX 78746 (512) 329-1076.

Texas Air Expo (*Waco*) Texas State Technical Institute hosts a aeronautic history demonstration. Displays feature aircraft from the world wars and state-of-the-art military technology. Air entertainment includes dog-fight reenactments, sky diving, and aerobatic performances such as the U. S. Air Force Thunderbirds. Generally held for a long weekend in mid-April. Texas Air Expo, Box 23333, **Waco**, TX 76702, (817) 752-9845.

MAY

Funfest (*Amarillo*) Three day extravaganza of family games and outdoor activities. Country and western entertainment, marathon, volleyball, golf, bike races. 1700 S. Polk, Amarillo, TX 79102-3154 (806) 374-0802.

Historic Homes Tour (*Galveston*) For two weekends in May several restored private homes in the East End and Silk Stocking Historic Districts are open to the public. Galveston Historical Foundation, 2016 Strand, **Galveston,** TX 77550, (409) 765-7834.

Historical Pilgrimage (*Jefferson*) Visit the gracious homes and spectacular gardens of the Old South at the peak of blossoming season. Parade and reenactment of the famous Diamond Bessie Murder Trial, an 1870's scandal that rocked the nation. Chamber of Commerce, 116 W. Austin, **Jefferson**, TX 75657, (214) 665-2672.

Laguna Gloria Fiesta (*Austin*) The largest juried art show in Texas has over 200 exhibitors selling and displaying their work. Entertainment, food, refreshments, art auction. Always the third weekend in May. Laguna Gloria Art Museum, 3809 W. 35th, **Austin**, TX 78703, (512) 458-8191.

Old Fiddlers' Reunion (*Athens*) Since 1933, fiddlers of all ages compete for prizes in several age categories. Jam sessions, bluegrass bands and street dances. Generally held the third weekend in May. P.O. Box 1441, **Athens**, TX 75851, (214) 675-1859.

Stagecoach Days (*Marshall*) A celebration of Marshall's history as a transportation hub with stagecoach rides, a trail ride and family entertainment. Chamber of Commerce, Box 520, **Marshall**, TX 75670, (214) 935-7868.

Texas State Arts and Crafts Fair (*Kerrville*) The heart of Hill Country is the setting for one of the state's best arts and crafts fairs where hundreds of Texas artisans and craftsmen exhibit and sell their wares. Live country and western and plenty of food. Texas Arts and Crafts Foundation, P.O. Box 1527, **Kerrville**, TX 78029-1527, (512) 896-5711.

JUNE

Chisholm Trail Roundup (*Fort Worth*) The Stockyards National Historic District features range games, trail rides and country and western music. Generally held the first or second weekend in June. Fort Worth Convention and Visitors Bureau, 100 E. 15th Street, Suite 400, **Fort Worth**, TX 76102, (817) 336-8791 or (800) 433-5747.

El Paso Street Festival (*El Paso*) This eight day event in late June honors the arts, music, history, food and culture of the border region. Convention and Visitors Bureau, 5 Civic Center Plaza, **El Paso**, TX 79901, (915) 534-0696.

Fiesta del Concho (*San Angelo*) Events along the shores of the Concho River include barge rides and balloon races. "Frontier Day" of the Fiesta demonstrates life in the 1880's including wagon rides, infantry drills and the Texas Sheep Shearing Contest. Convention and Visitors Bureau, 500 Rio Concho Drive, **San Angelo**, TX 76903, (915) 653-1206.

Peach Jamboree and Rodeo (Stonewall) The peach is Stonewall's prime crop and this event honors the fuzzy fruit with a parade, peach show and auction and live entertainment. Chamber of Commerce, Box 1, **Stonewall**, TX 78671, (512) 644-2735.

"TEXAS" The Historical Musical Drama (*Canyon*) This highly acclaimed musical, created by Pulitzer Prize winner Paul Green, brings the history of Texas to life. The cast of 80 performs beneath the mighty cliffs of Palo Duro Canyon on summer evenings from mid-June through late-August. Texas barbecue dinner available before the performance. "TEXAS" Historical Musical Drama, P.O. Box 268, Canyon, TX 79015, (806) 655-2181.

JULY

Aqua-Boom Celebration (*Kingsland*) Activities last for three days (including July 4) and take place in and around Lake LBJ. Jet-ski contest, water-ski show, raft race, parade. Chamber of Commerce, P.O. Box 465, **Kingsland**, TX 78639, (915) 388-6211

Bastille Day Celebration (*Paris*) Like its namesake, Paris, TX celebrates the Parisians assault of the Bastille prison on July 14. Reenactment of the fall of the Bastille, Tour de Paris bike race. Chamber of Commerce, P. O. Box 1096, **Paris**, TX 75461. (214) 784-2501.

Black-Eyed Pea Jamboree (*Athens*) Athens commemorates the prosperity that the famous black-eyed-pea has brought to the city making it the "Black-Eyed Pea Capital of the World". Events include pea popping, pea shelling, pea eating and a "reci-pea" contest. Third weekend in July. Chamber of Commerce, P.O. Box 2600 **Athens**, TX 75751 (214) 675-5181.

Borderfest (*Laredo*) This festival celebrates the Fourth of July and Laredo's cultural history under seven different flags. Parade, food, arts and crafts, entertainment. Laredo Convention and Visitors Bureau, P.O. Box 790, **Laredo**, TX 78042, (512) 722-9895.

Deep Sea Roundup (*Port Aransas*) The oldest fishing tournament on the Texas Coast. Prizes awarded for the biggest catch in several divisions. Early July. Chamber of Commerce, P.O. Box 356 **Port Aransas**, TX 78373 (512) 749-5919.

Great Texas Mosquito Festival (*Clute*) Competitions in honor of the mosquito include the Ms. Quito pageant, mosquito calling contest and the Mosquito Juice Chug-a Lug. Carnival, arts and crafts, family entertainment. Generally the third weekend in July. City Parks and Recreation, Box 997, **Clute**, TX 77531, (409) 265-8392.

Texas International Wine Classic (*Lubbock*) Tastings, seminars, competitions and exhibits of regional and international wines. Late September. P.O. Box 501, **Lubbock**, TX 79408 (806) 763-4666.

West of the Pecos Rodeo (*Pecos*) Dates back to 1883 when local cowboys got together to determine which ranch had the best steer ropers and bronco riders and is now credited as the world's first rodeo. Rodeo parade, dances, food and entertainment. Generally held over July 4. Chamber of Commerce, P.O. Box 27, **Pecos**, TX 79772, (915) 445-2406.

AUGUST

Gillespie County Fair (*Fredericksburg*) All of the expected Country Fair events plus dances on Friday and Saturday night make up Texas' "oldest continuous county fair." Fourth weekend in August. Chamber of Commerce, P.O. Box 506, **Fredericksburg**, TX 78624, (512) 997-2359.

National Sailplane Competiton (*Uvalde*) Sailplane pilots form all over the world gather for the excellent soaring weather in Uvalde. 10 days in mid-August. Chamber of Commerce, Box 706, **Uvalde**, TX (512) 278-3363.

North Texas State Fair (*Denton*) In addition to a fine livestock show, arts and crafts and country music, unusual highlights include a professional all-girl rodeo, miniature horse show and mule rodeo. Generally held the last full week of the month. North Texas Fairgrounds, P.O. Box 1695, **Denton**, TX 76202 (817) 387-2632.

Texas Folklife Festival (*San Antonio*) Annual celebration of Texas' cultural and ethnic diversity. Over 30 ethnic groups including Hungarians, Poles, Germans, Mexicans and Filipino's share their crafts, music, food, dance, culture and heritage. Entertainment. Generally held the first week in August. Institute of Texan Cultures, P.O. Box 1226, **San Antonio**, TX 78294, (512) 226-7651.

Westfest (*West*) Festive Czech celebration featuring dancing, parades, country and western music and foods by Czech and other ethnic groups. Always held the weekend before Labor Day. Westfest Inc, P.O. Box 65, **West**, TX 76691, (817) 826-5058.

XIT Rodeo and Reunion (*Dalhart*) Homecoming for the old XIT Ranch hands. The public is invited for rodeo, parades and free barbecue. Always held first weekend in August. Chamber of Commerce, P.O. Box 967, **Dalhart**, TX 79022, (806) 249-5646.

SEPTEMBER

"Come and Take It" Celebration (*Gonzales*) When Mexican soldiers tried to retrieve a cannon that had been loaned to the colonists, the armed citizenry challenged, "Come and take it". This three day event commemorates the first shots fired for Texas independence. Battle reenactment, frontier costumes, pioneer village and athletic competitions. Chamber of Commerce, Old Jail Museum, 414 St. Lawrence St, P.O. Box 134, **Gonzales**, TX 78629, (512) 672-6532.

National Championship Pow-Wow (*Grand Prairie*) This event brings together dozens of tribes from around the U. S. to compete in various dance categories in full dress regalia. Indian crafts, archery contest, tee-pee exhibit, Native American food booths. Always held the weekend after Labor Day. Traders Village, 2602 Mayfield, **Grand Prairie**, TX 75051, (214) 647-2331.

Permian Basin Fair and Exposition (*Odessa*) Traditional fair exhibits mixed with flower, commercial, auto, boat and motorcycle exhibits make this a very popular event. Mid-September. P. O. Box 4812, **Odessa**, TX 79760, (915) 332-9111.

Texas Forest Festival and Southern Hushpuppy Olympics (*Lufkin*) Honors the timber industry and its contribution to the area. Highlights include professional lumberjack competitions in chainsaw, axe chopping and axe throwing. Youth contests, food, entertainment and the famous hushpuppy cook-off. Chamber of Commerce, Box 1606, **Lufkin**, TX 75902, (409) 634-6644.

Western Horse Races & Barbecue (*Brackettville*) Amateur horse races with old-fashioned Western saddles have been held annually for over 30 years. Barbecue, western art exhibits and live country and western all set in frontier-style Alamo Village. Alamo Village, P.O. Box 528, **Brackettville**, TX 78832, (512) 563-2580.

World Championship Barbecued Goat Cook-Off (*Brady*) Contestants from the U. S. and abroad compete. Other activities include an arts and crafts fair, Great Goat Gallop, sheep dog trails and family entertainment. Chamber of Commerce, 101 East First Street, **Brady**, TX 76825, (915) 597-3491.

OCTOBER

Autumn Trails Festival (*Winnsboro*) Scenic routes through East Texas forest land offer spectacular foliage and a variety of special events. Saturdays and Sundays throughout October. Chamber of Commerce, 201 W. Broadway, **Winnsboro**, TX 75494, (214) 342-3666.

Heart O' Texas Fair & Rodeo (*Waco*) Large Texas fair including championship rodeo, livestock shows, farming exhibits, arts and crafts and entertainment. Early October. Heart of Texas Fair & Rodeo, P.O. Box 7581, **Waco**, TX 76710, (817) 776-1660.

Oktoberfest (*Fredericksburg*) Authentic German "bierhalle" is featured Friday night and lederhosen-clad "oompah" bands provide continuous entertainment throughout the weekend. Waltz contest, arts and crafts, German food booths and carnival. First weekend in

October. Chamber of Commerce, P.O. Box 506, **Fredericksburg**, TX 78624, (512) 997-6523.

State Fair of Texas (*Dallas*) This 100-year-old State Fair is one of the oldest and largest in the country. Over 3 million people enjoy the livestock expositions, shoot-outs, fashion shows and entertainment provided at the 14 day event. State Fair of Texas, P.O. Box 26010, **Dallas**, TX 75226, (214) 565-9931.

Texas Renaissance Festival (*Plantersville*) Music, drama and over 250 artisans in quaint Elizabethan village surroundings. Chariot races, mimes, jugglers and magicians. Texas Renaissance Festival, Inc., Rt.2, Box 650, **Plantersville**, TX 77363, (713) 356-2178.

Texas Rose Festival (*Tyler*) The "Rose Capital" proudly honors their flower with a rose parade, decorated floats and garden tour highlighting over 500 varieties. Texas symphony performances, antique doll and china exhibit. Chamber of Commerce, P.O. Box 390, **Tyler**, TX 75710, (214) 592-1661.

NOVEMBER

Candlelight Posada (*McAllen*) Christmas tree lighting, band concerts and ethnic foods mark the beginning of the holiday season on both sides of the border. Candlelight procession through the streets is an ancient Mexican tradition. Last weekend in November. Chamber of Commerce, Box 790, **McAllen**, TX 78502, (512) 682-2871.

Terlingua World Championship Chili Cook-Off (*Terlingua*) Thousands of people converge on this West Texas ghost town to sample the best "bowls of red" in the country. Entrants must qualify for the event but spectators are welcome to sample the goodies! First weekend in November. Terlingua Chamber of Commerce, P.O. Box 336, **Terlingua**, TX 79852, (915) 371-2320.

Texas Gathering of the Scottish Clans (*Salado*) Representatives from over 200 clans descend on this picturesque Central Texas town for bagpiping competitions, Highland games and a parade of tartans and bands. Central Texas Area Museum, P.O. Box 36, 1 Main Street, **Salado**, TX 76571, (817) 947-5232.

Wurstfest (*New Braunfels*) This German community celebrates the sausage-making season with family entertainment, polka music and German food and dancing. Contests, sporting events, museum exhibits. Chamber of Commerce, P.O. Box 311417, **New Braunfels**, TX 78131, (512) 625-2385.

DECEMBER

Christmas by the Sea (*South Padre Island*) No snow, but a pre-Christmas celebration featuring a lighted boat parade and a Solar Bear Swim ring in the holiday season. Tree lighting ceremony, caroling and concerts. Early December. Visitor and Convention Bureau, P.O. Box 3500, **South Padre Island**, TX 78597 (512) 761-6433.

Dickens on the Strand (*Galveston*) The Strand is transformed into Victorian London with street performers and vendors, carolers and characters from Dickens stories. Entertainment, food booths, parade. Generally held first weekend of the month. Galveston Historical Foundation, 2016 Strand, **Galveston**, TX 77550 (409) 765-7834.

Fiesta Navidena (*San Antonio*) Candlelight procession along the River Walk along with holiday food and pinata parties spread the holiday spirit. Two weeks before Christmas. Convention and Visitors Bureau, Box 2277, **San Antonio**, TX 78298, (512) 270-8700.

Winterfest (*Gonzales*) Turn-of-the-century entertainment, music and food celebrate the various cultures in Gonzales. First weekend in December. City Hall, P.O. Box 547, **Gonzales**, TX 78624 (512) 672-6532.

A FEW OF MY FAVORITE THINGS...

ELLIE RUCKER
Consumer Columnist
Austin American-Statesman

"In April, it's the bluebonnets! My favorite drives are Highway 290 East to Elgin from Austin and Highway 183 south toward Lockhart.

"In the summertime, it's the view of Lake Travis from the deck of the Oasis Bar and Restaurant. The decks hang from cliffs rising out of the lake.

"In the wintertime, at night, it's the view of the Capitol from the 8th floor of the Stokes Building Parking Garage at Guadalupe and 12th Streets. The Capitol is bathed in white light. Through bare oak branches, it's both eerie and beautiful.

"When I need a lift, I go to Whit Hanks at Treaty Oak—an antique store that resembles a middle–Eastern bazaar—a gathering of some of the most interesting antiques in Texas.

"Anytime of the year, I get chills driving over the new Loop 360 Bridge. It's really not new anymore but it still makes my heart sing to see it. Approaching it from either direction is like being in the peace, quiet and charm of the Hill Country without leaving the city limits of Austin."

PAUL SALOPEK
News Feature Writer
El Paso Times

"Visiting Franklin Mountain State Park where the desert mountain ranges look like shaved, sunburned heads jutting up from the ground.

"Crossing over to Juarez to visit the open market behind the main cathedral which offers a titillating shopping experience.

"Bar–hopping from the Dome Bar at the Westin El Paso del Norte Hotel to the Hollywood Care on S. El Paso Street. It's interesting to observe the socio–economic extremes from beveled glass and cool jazz to smoke-filled rooms and Nortena music."

KIMBERLY BAKER
Feature Writer
Amarillo Daily News

"The Indian art at the Panhandle Plains Historical Museum.

"Stanley Marsh's Cadillac Ranch featuring a collection of 1949–1960 fin–backed Cadillacs with the noses buried at a 40 degree angle. Great example of '70s pop art.

"It looks like 'The Best Little Whorehouse in Texas' from outside but Bob Lee's 'Big Texan' restaurant promises if you can finish the 72-oz steak within an hour, it's on the house."

FOOD *Continued from page 49*

Black-eyed peas, okra and fried chicken are among the favorites and are always prepared en masse. The most "Texan" of these southern delicacies is chicken-fried steak. Though it could have been first runner-up in the State Dish competition, it will never make the American Heart Association Hall of Fame. Chicken-fried steak is an inexpensive cut of beef pounded tender, dipped in thick batter and fried; it is never served without a creamy gravy made from the drippings and a generous portion of mashed potatoes. It dates back to frontier days and must have been the brain-child of a desperate chuck wagon cook who was afraid of the cowboys giving him over to the Indians if he served another tough piece of meat.

Texans, however, do not live by chicken-fried steak (or chili) alone. They engage is some more exciting libations as well. Beer goes very nicely with many of the regional dishes, and native Pearl and Lonestar—in long neck bottles—are just fine, thank you. For years Texans enjoyed "homebrew," but there's now a law on the books against concocting your own. However, in June of 1971, the law against serving liquor by the drink was repealed, so now there's no problem getting a potent margarita. Of course, only Yankees order them frozen with "No salt, please."

But the question remains: You have only one meal in Texas, what's it going to be? So many decisions to make, not to mention the heretofore unmentioned: Gulf shrimp, Gillespie County peaches and West Texas beef (well done, of course). Fortunately, the rest of the world has caught on to Lone Star cuisine, and there are great Tex-Mex joints from Brooklyn to Bimini. You can get nachos at O'Hare and pick up a bottle of Texas Best barbecue sauce at any Safeway. But ask a Texan for advice and he or she is sure to say, "Y'all come back now, y'hear!"

—*Mary T. Mulkerin*

You'd expect to find a wide variety of music in a state that is larger than France and more populous than Australia. Texas' music is as diverse as the state's geography, and the state has served as the stomping grounds for thousands of talented musicians. ⭐ Perhaps no other state in the union has provided popular music with as many musical trendsetters as has Texas. Buddy Holly, Willie Nelson, Roy Orbison, Ornette Coleman and Bob Wills are just a few of the many Texas natives who made indelible impressions on American popular music. These and other artists perfected their art in the halls and honky tonks of the state before going nationwide—and eventually worldwide—with their talents. ⭐ That legacy continues. During the 1980s, more than 70 Texas-based acts were signed to major-label recording contracts. Texas' latest chart-toppers, Edie Brickell and New Bohemians and Clint Black, are living proof that the Texas wellspring of talent is far from dry. ⭐ After all, as late as 1988 you could go to the Red Lion, a small club in Houston, and for little or no cover hear Clint Black playing for a few dozen people. He's since sold several million albums. If you're interested in discovering some of the stars of tomorrow today, here are the places to find them.

LIVE MUSIC ROUNDUP

WHERE TO FIND TOMORROW'S STARS TODAY

BY CASEY MONAHAN

Director of the Texas Music Office for the Texas Department of Commerce and former music writer for the Austin American–Statesman

AUSTIN

The state capital of Texas is also the state's music capital. Austin is widely recognized as one of the finest live music towns in the world, one that supports its musicians and the music halls where they ply their trade. On nearly any weekend night, between 80 and 100 musical acts can be found in clubs in and around this Hill Country city. With such an astounding amount of live music available, and with approximately 700,000 people residing in the three-county area, there is more live music per capita in Austin than anywhere else in America.

From country to jazz, rock and roll to rap, conjunto to classical, most any musical style is available. The following venues are some of the city's finest:

ANTONE'S: "Austin's Home of the Blues" was founded in 1975 by Clifford Antone, a Port Arthur native who, like so many former University of Texas ex-students, came to Austin to go to college and never left. More a patron of the art of blues music than a club owner, Antone has brought such legends as Clifton Chenier, Muddy Waters, Willie Dixon and Big Joe Turner to his stage. He's also played a pivotal role in nurturing native Texas talents such as Stevie Ray Vaughan and Double Trouble and the Fabulous Thunderbirds on their way to international fame. Call (512) 474-5314 for information.

BROKEN SPOKE: One of the last authentic Texas dance halls found in a major Texas city, the Broken Spoke was recently selected by *Texas Highways* as one of the finest honky tonks in Texas. Bob Wills and Ernest Tubb are among the many country stars who've played the 'Spoke, and it's not unusual to find Willie Nelson sitting in for an impromptu set with whoever is performing. Besides featuring a huge dance floor, the Broken Spoke is also a restaurant, with southern style food as its main fare. Call (512) 442-6189 for information.

EAST SIXTH STREET: What is popularly called Austin's version of New Orleans' Bourbon Street is actually an eight-block section of downtown frequented on weekends by college students and young adults. More than 20 of the restored 19th century storefronts are live music clubs. Five emphasize original music: the Black Cat Lounge (no phone), a low-frills, beer-only bar showcasing country, rock and blues acts; Chicago House (512-473-2542), an intimate, acoustic-only venue featuring singer/songwriters as well as small theatrical productions; Steamboat (512-478-2913), a large, split-level showcase featuring the town's biggest draws; Red River Saloon (512-482-9272), a country and blues bar; and the Cannibal Club (512-472-2002), a hub of Austin's burgeoning alternative rock and roll scene. Other venues on East Sixth range from lively Top 40 cover band bars to trendy discoteques.

ELSEWHERE IN AUSTIN: Other prominent live music locales include the Continental Club (512-441-2444), Blue Bayou (512-445-7544), Liberty Lunch (512-477-0461), Hole in the Wall (512-472-5599), the Texas Tavern (512-471-5651), the Cactus Cafe (512-471-8228), La Zona Rosa (512-482-0662) and the Lumberyard (512-255-4073). Forty miles south of Austin in Gruene (pronounced Green) is the one of the oldest (and certainly one of the finest) dancehalls in the state, Gruene Hall (512-629-5077).

For music listings, venue addresses and phone numbers, consult the Thursday entertainment section of the *Austin American-Statesman*, the city's daily newspapers, the free weekly, the *Austin Chronicle*, or the *Music City News*, a free monthly.

DALLAS/FORT WORTH

Since the mid-'80s, Dallas has developed a vibrant live music scene of its own. The Deep Ellum area east of downtown is Dallas' musical hub, with a wide variety of music halls located in or near this area. Prominent venues include Club Da Da (214-744-3232), with an eclectic booking policy focusing on original music from Dallas and Austin; the Arcadia Theatre (214-826-7554), which books mostly touring acts that run the range between Lyle Lovett and the Gunbunnies; Club Clearview (214-701-3501) featuring mostly local acts that emphasize the industrial or avante garde edge of rock; Poor David's Pub (214-821-9891), a 13-year-old club featuring mostly blues, folk, zydeco and and country acts; the Sons of Hermann Hall (214-747-4422), a traditional country and folk venue; and the Video Bar (214-939-9113), which is dedicated to post modern avante garde video with a weekly showcase of eclectic local music. Also located near downtown is Dallas Alley (214-988-9378), a collection of nine clubs (five featuring a variety of live music) and a large outdoor pavillion featuring roadshows and top local draws.

Fort Worth, located 30 minutes west of Dallas, has several quality live music locations to choose from, including the upscale Caravan of Dreams (817-429-4000), one of the finest places to hear music in Texas; Billy Bob's Texas (817-624-7117), a quintessential Texas dancehall of enormous proportions; J&J's Blues Bar (817-870-2337), which features local and regional blues talent; and the White Elephant Saloon (817-624-9712), a traditional Texas hang out catering to country and acoustic acts.

For information on who's playing where and when, pick up a free copy of the *Dallas Observer*, the local arts and entertainment weekly.

HOUSTON

The home of rock group ZZ Top is also the home of an increasingly active live music scene. Country, rhythm and blues and rock and roll dominate, although unlike Dallas and Austin, there is no one area of the city with a high concentration of live music acts.

Although Gilley's, the Beaumont honky tonk made famous by the movie *Urban Cowboy*, was temporarily closed in March of '89, there are still plenty of good venues available featuring live country or folk music. Sure-fire country picks include the Chip Kicker (713-440-8882), a two-story club featuring live country music seven nights a week; Eddie's Country Ballroom (713-489-8181), located just south of Houston in Manvel, is a gigantic, family-oriented live country music dancehall; the Wunsche Bros. Saloon and Cafe (713-353-2825) is a combination country, rock and blues bar, and restaurant; Anderson Fair (713-528-8576), which has touring folk acts every weekend; and the Red Lion (713-795-5000), a restaurant with an upstairs bar that presents acoustic music.

More urban selections are Rudyard's (713-521-0521), a college rock and roll bar; Axiom (713-224-1420), an all-ages, post-punk venue; Rockefeller's (713-861-9365) which features top regional and national club acts; Club Hey Hey (713-863-3732), mixing zydeco, roots rock and blues in an authentic setting; and Fitzgerald's (713-862-3838), which mixes alternative rock, world beat and blues.

For information about live music in and around Houston, pick up a free copy of the *Houston Press*, the city's arts and entertainment weekly guide, or check listings in the *Public News*, a free arts, politics and entertainment weekly.

SAN ANTONIO

The Alamo City is best known as the unofficial capital of Conjunto, the native Texas musical genre that developed around the turn of the century when Texas Hispanics adapted the German push-button accordian into their native Tex-Mex folk music. A main Tex-Mex locale is the Desparado Club (512-680-7225), with Tejano masters performing on any given weekend. Other Tex-Mex venues include Randy's Ballroom (512-434-6266) and Reflex (512-737-5900).

The premiere folk and country club is the Leon Springs Cafe (512-698-3338). Best bets for rock and roll and pop are: Rick's (512-732-9118), featuring mostly local and regional rock and roll and funk acts; St. Mary's Bar and Grill (512-737-3900), a blues and rock bar just off the campus of St. Mary's University; Tycoon Flats (512-737-1929), a folk, blues and rock bar with a comfortable patio and food; Irie's (512-699-6313), a rock, reggae and blues venue with a splendid open air area; Panama Red's (713-732-1005), San Antonio's newest rock and roll club; Monterrey Jack's (512-496-8055), a top 40 cover band bar; and La Playa (512-737-1005) a slightly upscale Top 40 venue.

For information about live music in and around San Antonio, pick up a free copy of the *Current*, San Antonio's arts and entertainment weekly.

ANNUAL FESTIVALS

SOUTH BY SOUTHWEST MUSIC AND MEDIA CONFERENCE: Held over a five-day period in Austin during the middle of March, the conference includes the Austin Music Awards, and the four-night South By Southwest Music Festival. The latter presents more than 400 up-and-coming acts from around the country (with approximately half from Austin) performing in 22 music halls. Ostensibly a supermarket of bands playing for record company talent scouts, it's also an excellent opportunity to hear a tremendous amount of live music in a very short time. For information, call (512) 477-7979.

⭐

KERRVILLE FOLK FESTIVAL: Begun in 1972 by Rod Kennedy, the Kerrville Folk Festival is the largest and longest running folk festival in Texas. Over an 18-day period beginning Memorial Day weekend, Kennedy's Quiet Valley Ranch (located nine miles south of Kerrville) is transformed into an open-air concert hall that features acts such as Shawn Colvin, Peter Yarrow, Gary P. Nunn, Tom Paxton, David Amram and Butch Hancock. Perhaps even more renowned than the evening concerts are the informal late night campfire jams, when performers play to all hours of the night. For information, call (512) 257-3600.

⭐

TEJANO CONJUNTO FESTIVAL: Begun in 1981 by the Guadalupe Cultural Arts Center as a means of providing greater recognition and support for Conjunto music in Texas, this festival has blossomed into one of the top ten ethnic festivals in the United States. Held annually in San Antonio during the second weekend in May, the six-day festival brings together some of the top Conjunto acts in Texas for workshops and concert performances. Ruben Vela, Flaco Jimenez, Esteban Jordan, Tony De La Rosa and Valerio Longoria are just a few of the Texas legends who regularly play the festival. Besides the sweet sounds of the push-button squeeze box accordian, there are arts and crafts booths and some of the best Mexican food in the state. For information, call (512) 271-3151.

⭐

OTHER ANNUAL FESTIVALS AND EVENTS: There are more than 100 county fairs, rodeos and festivals held annually around the state that include live music; contact the Texas Music Office for a list or for any additional information about Texas music. Its address is Post Office Box 12728, Austin, Texas 78711, or call (512) 320-9562.